Complying with the ADA

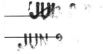

WILEY SMALL BUSINESS EDITIONS

Jeffrey G. Allen, *Complying with the ADA: A Small Business Guide to Hiring and Employing the Disabled*

Kim Baker and Sunny Baker, *How to Promote, Publicize, and Advertise Your Growing Business*

Daryl Allen Hall, *1001 Businesses You Can Start from Home*

Herman Holtz, *How to Start and Run a Writing and Editing Business*

John Kremer, *The Complete Direct Marketing Sourcebook: A Step-by-Step Guide to Organizing and Managing a Successful Direct Marketing Program*

Harold J. McLaughlin, *The Entrepreneur's Guide to Building a Better Business Plan: A Step-by-Step Approach*

Richard L. Porterfield, *The Insider's Guide to Winning Government Contracts*

OTHER BOOKS BY JEFFREY G. ALLEN

How to Turn an Interview into a Job
(also available on audiocassette)

Finding the Right Job at Midlife

The Placement Strategy Handbook

The Employee Termination Handbook

Placement Management

Surviving Corporate Downsizing

The Complete Q&A Job Interview Book

The Perfect Job Reference

The National Placement Law Center Fee Collection Guide

The Perfect Follow-Up Method to Get the Job

Jeff Allen's Best: The Resume

Jeff Allen's Best: Get the Interview

Jeff Allen's Best: Win the Job

Complying with the ADA

A Small Business Guide to Hiring and Employing the Disabled

Jeffrey G. Allen, J.D., C.P.C.

John Wiley & Sons, Inc.
New York • Chichester • Brisbane • Toronto • Singapore

This publication is designed to provide accurate and authoritative
information in regard to the subject matter covered. It is sold with
the understanding that the publisher is not engaged in rendering
legal, accounting, or other professional service. If legal advice or
other expert assistance is required, the services of a competent
professional person should be sought. From a *Declaration of
Principles jointly adopted by a Committee of the American Bar
Association and a Committee of Publishers.*

Library of Congress Cataloging-in-Publication Data:

Allen, Jeffrey G., 1943–
    Complying with the ADA : a small business guide to hiring and
employing the disabled / by Jeffrey G. Allen.
        p.   cm.—(Wiley small business editions)
    "A small business guide to the new Disabilities Act."
    Includes bibliographical references and index.
    ISBN 0-471-59049-5 (cloth).—ISBN 0-471-59051-7 (paper)
    1. Handicapped—Employment—United States.   2. Employee
selection—United States.   3. Handicapped—Employment—Law
and legislation—United States.   I. Title.   II. Series.
HD7256.U5A683   1993
658.3'045—dc20   92-34801

Printed in the United States of America

10   9   8   7   6   5   4   3   2   1

Dedicated to changing the phrase *reasonable accommodation* to real *acceptance*.

With appreciation ...

To my wife, Bev;
to our daughter, Angela;
to an editor's editor, Mike Hamilton;
to his assistant, Elena Paperny; and
to Pat Stahl,
    the most capable researcher any author could want.

Thanks more than words can say.

Preface

Disabled, handicapped, impaired. Translation: "crippled." Words that describe people negatively; words that are synonymous in the work world with *unqualified, incompetent, expensive,* or worse—such reflexive stereotypes automatically exclude almost *one-third* of our work force!

Yet experience teaches us that people with physical or mental weaknesses in certain areas often compensate with strengths in others. People who cannot hear generally see better. Those with poor eyesight hear better. Amputees develop greater strength in their remaining limbs. These aren't isolated cases. They are examples of the natural adaptive process that has existed since the first life forms evolved.

Unfortunately, discrimination against the disabled can be traced back almost as far; it probably began the day the first job was created.

For all of the equal employment opportunity legislation of the past 25 years, there has been almost no affirmative action to hire the disabled. This is largely due to their "invisibility."

Despite the fact that I spent 24 years as a recruiter, personnel consultant, human resources manager, and employment lawyer, and that I was the author of more than a dozen books about the hiring process, I never realized the obstacles that the disabled encounter until I broke my hip.

Instantly I noticed how inaccessible everything was—my car, a restaurant, an office building. Moving around was also difficult. I couldn't even find a comfortable place to sit.

The temporary inconvenience I experienced during my convalescence was nothing compared with what people with permanent impairments face every day. Despite their sometimes amazing adaptations, they have been physically and psychologically blocked from the mainstream of our society.

If you doubt it, just check the disabled area in any parking lot. The chances are better than 50 percent that some unauthorized car is there. The fines are stiff, but it's so convenient. Even legally designated, strictly enforced, specially designed areas yield to expediency. Who really knows another's pain? And, too often, who really cares?

Federal law leveled the playing field for disabled job seekers and employees on July 26, 1992, when the employment provisions of the Americans with Disabilities Act (ADA) became the law of the land. The ADA is a sweeping federal mandate that authorizes administrative, civil, and criminal penalties for discriminating against the disabled with respect to "job application procedures, hiring, advancement, discharge, compensation, job training and other terms, conditions and privileges of employment."

The mandate has the potential to revolutionize the hiring and employment process permanently. It affects everything from preemployment screening (testing, evaluating qualifications, interviewing, etc.) to physical workplace alterations. Most regulations are general; and key concepts in the law such as "essential functions" and "readily achievable" are not precisely defined, leaving major ambiguities that will undoubtedly be the basis of endless administrative and judicial review.

If you have more than 25 employees in your organization, you are liable. The minimum will be reduced to 15 employees on July 26, 1994. Nobody's perfect—everyone is a potential claimant.

As a small businessperson, you are particularly vulnerable to claims by applicants and employees because you probably don't know the many technical nuances of the law. Large corporations have human resources professionals on staff, legal counsel in house, and outside consultants or trainers available to assist in this major undertaking, but many private entrepreneurs have to go it alone. Even if you have the money and time to seek outside assistance, few attorneys and human resources professionals really understand application of the mandates.

The Equal Employment Opportunity Commission (EEOC) and your state compliance authority are inadequate to assist as well. This year the number of complaints from the ADA alone should increase their work load by 25 percent. Even before the ADA, equal employment compliance agencies were inaccessible, understaffed, and inefficient. Those that functioned at all, assumed an adversarial position to employers. Once you are targeted, the government's unlimited power to investigate and prosecute is brought to bear on your business.

This book is written to help small business owners understand their obligations under the ADA. It doesn't answer every question about the law because some issues are still being decided, but it does offer my best judgments based on my reading of the law, the accompanying regulations, and available research. It will guide you through the basics of the law and point you to the myriad other resources available on this subject. I've included sample job applications, model position descriptions, checklists, and case studies to illustrate specific applications.

The book is divided into two broad sections. Part One, Hiring the Disabled, covers recruitment, interviewing, testing, compensation, training, and other issues involved in hiring. Part Two, Employing the Disabled, offers accessibility guidelines to help you accommodate your employees and customers.

I hope the book will motivate you not only to make a good faith effort to comply with the *letter* of the law, but to respond in the *spirit* of the law by taking an "affirmative action" to work with people who are technically "disabled."

Use it well!

JEFFREY G. ALLEN, J.D., C.P.C.

Beverly Hills, California

About the Author

Jeffrey G. Allen, J.D., C.P.C., is America's leading employment attorney. For almost a decade, Mr. Allen was a human resources manager with small business employers or small divisions of major employers. This direct experience has been coupled with his employment law practice over the past 17 years. As a certified placement counselor, certified employment specialist, and professional negotiator, Mr. Allen is highly qualified to write the first book for entrepreneurs on hiring and employing the disabled.

Mr. Allen is the author of more bestselling books in the employment field than anyone else. Among them are *How to Turn an Interview into a Job, Finding the Right Job at Midlife, The Employee Termination Handbook, The Placement Strategy Handbook, Placement Management, The Complete Q&A Job Interview Book, The Perfect Job Reference, The Perfect Follow-Up Method to Get the Job*, and the popular three-book series *Jeff Allen's Best*. He writes a nationally syndicated column entitled "Placements and The Law," conducts seminars, and is regularly featured in television, radio, and newspaper interviews.

Mr. Allen has served as Director of the National Placement Law Center, Special Advisor to the American Employment Association, General Counsel to the California Association of Personnel Consultants, judge pro tem, and is recognized as the nation's foremost employment attorney.

Contents

Introduction

IS THE ADA GOOD FOR BUSINESS?

On July 20, 1990, President Bush fulfilled a campaign promise by signing into law the Americans with Disabilities Act (ADA), regarded by many as the most sweeping piece of legislation since the Civil Rights Act of 1964. While many advocacy groups for the disabled hail it as the "emancipation proclamation of the disabled," many employers are understandably apprehensive about its legal and economic implications for their business: What will it cost to comply?

The new law will require changes in the way businesses and public facilities operate. Some of these changes will be physical and will cost money; others will involve adopting new attitudes toward people with disabilities. But creating equal access for the nation's disabled is not just a moral or legal obligation. It is also good business. To put the potential benefits of the law into perspective, consider these work force projections from the U.S. Department of Labor:

- White men, for decades the majority of workers, will make up only 45 percent of the total work force by the year 2000.

- Women, minorities, and immigrants will account for more than 80 percent of the U.S. labor force growth in the year 2000.

- The growth rate of the labor force in the year 2000 will be only 1.2 percent, compared with an annual growth rate of 2.6 percent in the

1

1970s. In 1995, the number of Americans 18 to 24 years of age will bottom out at a little under 24 million, compared with a peak of 30 million in 1980.

• One out of three people will be 50 years of age or older by the turn of the century. The largest age group of workers will be those who are 35 to 54 years old.

What do these changes mean? Because of projected labor shortages, previously underutilized segments of the labor force, such as women, minorities, elderly, and disabled workers, will be actively recruited by business and industry.

There are an estimated 43 million disabled Americans, more than 60 percent of whom are unemployed. The cost of maintaining people with disabilities who cannot find jobs has increased steadily over the past 20 years. In 1970, total disability expenditures amounted to $19.3 billion. By 1986, they increased by 779 percent to $169.4 billion. The federal government now spends about $200 billion a year on direct public and private assistance for people with disabilities. This includes Social Security disability insurance, supplemental security income, worker's compensation, welfare, and private transfer payments that reflect claims of people injured on the job. Add another $1 billion for lost taxes and lost production and you begin to see the economic wisdom of employing the disabled.

One Company's Experience

Kreonite, a manufacturer of darkroom equipment in Wichita, Kansas, with $30 million a year in sales, hired its first disabled workers 20 years ago, and two of that first group are still there. Today, people with cerebral palsy, mental retardation, mental illness, and various sensory impairments make up 15 percent of the company's work force of 240. The company says it is motivated by business needs, not altruism, to hire disabled workers and, according to a recent article in *The New York Times* (July 27, 1992), its experience with them has been overwhelmingly positive.[1]

Wichita has a low unemployment rate of around 4 percent and is home to several big aircraft makers that can pay skilled workers more

[1]Peter Kilborn, "Company Invests in Human Assets: Disabled Employees in Regular Jobs." *The New York Times*, 27 July 1992, A8.

than Kreonite does, so workers are hard to find. In the 1980s, the company was losing one in every three production workers a year, at a turnover cost of about $1,000 per worker. Partly as a result of hiring more disabled workers and accommodating them better, Kreonite's annual rate of turnover is down to one in ten—a big savings for the company.

The lesson of Kreonite is that disabled people represent a large untapped resource of qualified labor. The ADA will help businesses gain access to this labor pool while giving qualified workers greater access to business.

LEGISLATIVE HISTORY OF THE ADA

The ADA extends civil rights protection to people with disabilities that are parallel to those established by the federal government for women and minorities. It is essentially an amalgam of two major civil rights statutes: the Civil Rights Act of 1964 and the Rehabilitation Act of 1973. The ADA uses the framework of Titles II and VII of the Civil Rights Act of 1964 for coverage and enforcement, and the framework of the Rehabilitation Act of 1973 for defining disability and determining what constitutes discrimination.

But whereas the Rehabilitation Act prohibited only those doing business with the federal government or receiving federal financial assistance from discriminating against qualified individuals with handicaps (the term used under that law), the ADA reaches into the private sector as well, affecting both large and small businesses.

Another significant difference between the ADA and its predecessor laws is that the ADA does not merely prohibit discrimination, as does Title VII of the Civil Rights Act, but imposes additional affirmative obligations upon businesses to accommodate the needs of people with disabilities and to promote their economic independence.

Since enacting the Rehabilitation Act of 1973, Congress has passed several other statutes prohibiting discrimination against individuals with disabilities. In addition to the federal laws, more than 40 states have their own laws protecting individuals with disabilities. The scope of protection under these laws varies greatly on such issues as coverage of private sector employers, the number of employers covered, and the obligation to make reasonable accommodation.

In congressional hearings on the ADA, former attorney general Richard Thornburgh argued that this new law weaves together the torn patchwork of existing federal and state legislation regarding people with disabilities and closes gaps in coverage.

Certain key terms are not defined in the law itself, so Congress directed the Equal Employment Opportunity Commission to issue comprehensive regulations clarifying the employment provisions of Title I in the ADA, and the attorney general of the United States to issue comprehensive regulations interpreting the public accommodations provisions of Title III in the ADA. These regulations are extremely useful in interpreting the ADA.

OVERVIEW OF TITLES I THROUGH V

Although this book is concerned primarily with employment issues, the ADA prohibits both intentional and unintentional discrimination in five broad areas, some of which touch upon employment.

Title I: Employment. A key provision of the ADA is the prohibition of discrimination against individuals with disabilities in public-and private-sector employment. Title VII of the Civil Rights Act of 1964 opened the doors of American business to minorities and women. Title I of the ADA offers the same promise to qualified individuals with disabilities. It requires employers to take immediate action to provide "reasonable accommodations" to both employees and job applicants for a broad range of mental and physical disabilities.

Title II: State and local governments and public services. This title prohibits public entities from discriminating against qualified individuals with disabilities or excluding them from participating in their services, programs, or activities. The ADA's guarantee of full participation in the mainstream of American life is illusory if accessible transportation is not available; hence, most of Title II's provisions deal with transportation provided to the general public via bus, rail, taxis, and limousines. Aircraft are excluded.

All new public buses must be accessible to persons with disabilities. Transit authorities must provide supplementary or special services to those who cannot use fixed-route bus services. New over-the-road buses, new rail vehicles, and all new rail stations must be accessible. Existing rail systems must have one accessible car per train within the next five years.

Title III: Public accommodations and services operated by private entities. Title III prohibits discrimination against individuals with disabilities in the full and equal enjoyment of the goods, services, facilities, and privileges of any place of public accommodation. It requires that the above benefits be offered "in the most integrated setting appropriate to the needs of the individual," except when the individual poses a direct threat to the health or safety of others.

Public accommodations include a broad range of entities, from airports to zoos. They extend to sales, rental, and service establishments as well as educational institutions, recreational facilities, and social service centers. Title III requires public accommodations to modify their policies and procedures and to provide auxiliary aids to disabled people unless doing so would fundamentally alter the nature of the organization or cause an undue burden. All newly constructed and substantially renovated buildings must be readily accessible to people with disabilities. Existing facilities must be made accessible if changes are "readily achievable."

Title IV: Telecommunications. Title IV ensures that individuals with disabilities will be able to communicate electronically. It requires that, within three years, telephone companies must provide telecommunications relay services that enable hearing-and speech-impaired individuals to communicate with hearing individuals through the use of telecommunications devices for the deaf (TDD) and other nonvoice terminal devices.

Title V: Miscellaneous provisions. In general, this title delineates the ADA's relationship to other laws, outlines insurance issues, and explains how each title in the act will be implemented. Title V prohibits retaliation against individuals who try to enforce their own rights under the ADA and amends the Rehabilitation Act of 1973 to exclude current users of alcohol and drugs from its coverage. It provides that nothing in the ADA shall be construed to apply to a lesser standard than the standards set in any other federal or state law as long as the previous law provides greater or equal protection.

ADA IMPLEMENTATION SCHEDULE

Title I. Employment

Employers of 25 or more people.	July 26, 1992.
Employers of 15 to 24 people.	July 26, 1994.
Employers of fewer than 15 people.	Law does not apply.

Title II. Transportation

Public transportation.	New stations built after January 26, 1992, must be accessible; one car per train must be accessible by July 26, 1995.
Rail transportation.	By July 26, 1995, Amtrak coaches must have one accessible car per train, and coaches must have some accessible seats; by July 26, 2000, coaches must have same number of accessible seats that they would have had if they had been built accessible.

Title III. Public Accommodations

Businesses with 25 or fewer employees and revenues of $1 million or less.	January 26, 1992.
Businesses with 10 or fewer employees and revenues of $500,000 or less.	January 26, 1993.

Title IV. Telecommunications

Telecommunications relay services to operate 24 hours a day.	July 26, 1993.

Title V. Miscellaneous

Effective dates of Title V.	Determined by analogous sections in Titles I through IV.

PART ONE

Hiring the Disabled

CHAPTER ONE

The Scope
of Title I

WHO IS REGULATED?

The Americans with Disabilities Act (ADA) ban on employment discrimination against people with disabilities applies to:

- Private employers
- Employment agencies
- Labor organizations
- Joint labor-management groups

As of July 26, 1992, Title I applies only to entities employing 25 or more people. As of July 26, 1994, it will extend to employers of 15 or more people. Firms with fewer than 15 employees are exempt from coverage altogether.

Because the ADA applies to employers and unions, new contracts between management and unions should provide standards for dealing with disabled job applicants and employees. Figure 1.1 contains sample contract language developed by the International Association of Machinists and Aerospace Workers Union.

Figure 1.1 Sample Union Contract Language

1. Nondiscrimination. The employer shall not discriminate against any employees covered by this agreement on the basis of disability, race, gender, religious belief, sexual preference, or national origin.

2. Job retention. Both parties to this agreement will work cooperatively to retain in employment a worker who becomes disabled on or off the job. Both parties also agree to work together to facilitate the individual's return to work as soon as possible.

3. Reasonable accommodation. It will be the policy of [*name of employer*] to make reasonable accommodations for the known limitations of a worker who has a disability. Such accommodations may include, but are not limited to, such things as workstation modification; making building facilities such as restrooms, cafeterias, or other facilities accessible; adaptation of tools and equipment, work schedules, and travel/transportation adjustment. The employee with a disability who is affected will be consulted on an accommodation. Any accommodation made will assure that the work will be performed safely.

4. Retraining and/or transfer of employee. It shall be the policy of [*name of employer*] that if an employee injured on or off the job is unable to return to his or her present job, the employer and the union will work together to make every effort to place the worker in another position for which he or she is qualified or can be qualified through training or accommodation.

5. Promotion. It shall be the policy of [*name of employer*] that promotions will be based on the ability to do the job and merit. This policy will apply to all employees, including those who have disabilities. Disability alone shall not be grounds for excluding a candidate from consideration.

6. Joint labor-management committee on workers with disabilities. To enhance the productivity of workers with disabilities and provide an opportunity for their full participation in employment-related and employer-sponsored activities, a joint labor-management committee on workers with disabilities shall be established. The committee's function will be to keep track of problems and recommend solutions as well as to review company policies and programs, and recommend any necessary changes.

Source: From the *Employer's Guide to the Americans with Disabilities Act* by James G. Frierson. Copyright © 1992, by The Bureau of National Affairs, Inc., Washington, DC 20037. Reprinted with permission.

POSTING REQUIREMENTS

All employers and organizations subject to the ADA must post notices in an accessible format and in an area where they are likely to be seen by job applicants and current employees. The new Consolidated EEO Poster, which meets the requirements of the ADA, is available from the Equal Employment Opportunity Commission (EEOC). Call 800-USA-EEOC.

WHO IS PROTECTED?

Title I of the ADA prohibits discrimination in any terms or conditions of employment for "qualified individuals with disabilities" and for people who have a known association or relationship with a disabled individual. Employers must base their hiring decisions on an applicant's ability to perform the job, not on the person's disability. Title I also has a proactive requirement that employers must "reasonably accommodate" individuals with disabilities. To comply with the ADA, you must determine:

- The essential functions of the job.
- Whether the person with a disability, with or without accommodation, is qualified to perform these duties.
- Whether a reasonable accommodation that does not constitute an undue hardship can be made for a qualified individual.

We shall explore these points in more detail in later chapters, but for now let's look at what is prohibited under Title I and what these provisions mean for you as a small business owner.

WHO ARE THE DISABLED?

As defined by the ADA, a disabled person is one who has a physical or mental impairment that substantially limits a major life activity, has a record of an impairment, or is regarded as having an impairment. Let's analyze each point in the definition.

1. *Has a physical or mental impairment that substantially limits one or more major life activities.* The term *impairment* includes any physiological disorder, cosmetic disfigurement, or anatomical loss as

well as any mental or psychological disorder. While there is no inclusive list of impairments, the ADA does give examples such as: acquired immunodeficiency syndrome (AIDS) and human immunodeficiency virus (HIV), alcoholism, cancer, cerebral palsy, diabetes, emotional illness, epilepsy, hearing and speech disorders, heart disease, certain learning disabilities such as dyslexia, mental retardation, muscular dystrophy, and visual impairments.

Some disabilities are obvious, others are not. This in no way affects your obligations as an employer under the ADA as long as you are aware of the disability.

Some physical conditions are not covered by the ADA. Individuals who are currently abusing drugs or alcohol are not protected by the ADA. The act also excludes simple physical characteristics such as eye color, hair color, height, or weight, and environmental, cultural, or economic circumstances such as poverty or homosexuality. The ADA does not recognize transitory conditions such as pregnancy and broken bones, even though they may, for a time, substantially limit a major life activity.

A *major life activity* is a basic function such as caring for oneself, walking, talking, seeing, hearing, speaking, breathing, sitting, standing, lifting, reaching, learning, and working. The term also includes cognitive functions such as learning, reasoning, and remembering.

With regard to the major life activity of working, the term *substantially limited* means that an individual is restricted in the ability to perform either a class of jobs or a broad range of jobs in various classes. The inability to perform a single, particular job is not a substantial limitation in the major life activity of working.

2. *Has a record of impairment.* This second prong of the definition protects people who had a disability in the past; for example, an individual with cancer in remission or a laborer with a history of back injuries. Anyone who has a past record of an impairment that restricts a major life activity is considered disabled even though the impairment does not currently cause a limitation. This includes rehabilitated drug addicts and recovering alcoholics.

One reason for covering people with a record of past impairment is to acknowledge that a person with a disabling condition does not cease to be disabled just because treatment alleviates the condition.

3. *Is regarded as having an impairment.* Also considered disabled are people who have no actual physical or mental impairment but who

15 STEPS TO COMPLIANCE

1. Update existing job descriptions or develop new ones that outline essential job functions.
2. Post notices describing the applicable provisions of the Americans with Disabilities Act.
3. Develop a corporate policy on discrimination against people with disabilities.
4. Review the architectural structure of your facility; evaluate accessibility of public areas and personnel department.
5. Educate employees involved in the hiring process about the requirements of the law.
6. Educate all employees about people with disabilities to promote understanding and acceptance of coworkers.
7. Consider designating someone to serve as the company's ADA information specialist.
8. Review all preemployment programs and eliminate preoffer medical-related questions or tests.
9. Determine if postoffer medical exams should be required for any jobs. Work with medical personnel to develop a format that will give you the information you need to make a fair placement decision.
10. Review existing contracts and leases, including collective bargaining agreements.
11. Conduct a self-audit of possible accommodations that your company could provide to a disabled employee.
12. Develop policies and procedures for reasonable accommodation; inform employees and applicants of their responsibility to let you know that they need accommodation.
13. Review return-to-work policies for newly disabled employees to ensure that accommodations are considered.
14. Document any accommodations made, as well as hiring and firing decisions.
15. Consider meeting with advocacy groups for individuals with disabilities to obtain advice and assistance.

are viewed by others as disabled. An example is a burn victim. Although the person may never have experienced any permanent physical or mental limitations, the scars may create an impression of disability. That person cannot be discriminated against because of an employer's fear that customers will react negatively to his or her appearance. This provision attempts to keep irrational assumptions from entering into employment decisions. It also applies to people with hearing problems, epilepsy, and other problems.

It is a good rule of thumb to base all hiring, placement, and salary decisions on the individual rather than on the type of disability. Like all workers, disabled people vary greatly in personality, intelligence, skill, and job performance. Keep in mind also that each person's impairment is different, even if the medical diagnosis is the same.

A final word about who is disabled: When thinking about the ADA, don't think only in terms of hiring practices. In fact, most disabled workers will become disabled *after* they are employed. Accidents, diabetes, heart conditions, and other disabilities are most likely to occur when one is an adult and already on the job. With this in mind, try to identify current employees who are disabled so that reasonable accommodations can be made to allow them to work at peak efficiency. See Chapter 6 for suggestions on disability management.

CHAPTER TWO

Areas of Regulation in the ADA

IN WHAT AREAS OF EMPLOYMENT IS DISCRIMINATION PROHIBITED?

An employer may not discriminate against a qualified individual with a disability in any part of the employment process. The Americans with Disabilities Act (ADA) specifically mentions the following areas:

- Job application procedures: recruiting, advertising, and processing of applications.
- Hiring, upgrading, promotion; tenure, demotion, transfer, layoff, termination, right of return from layoff, and rehiring.
- Rates of pay and other forms of compensation.
- Job assignments, job classifications, organizational structures, position descriptions, lines of progression, and seniority lists.
- Leaves of absence, sick leave, and other leaves.
- Fringe benefits, whether or not they are administered by the employer.
- Training, including apprenticeships, professional meetings, and related activities.
- Employer-sponsored activities, including social or recreational programs.

As with other civil rights laws prohibiting discrimination in employment, the ADA does not negate an employer's right to choose and maintain a qualified work force. This means that you can continue to use job-related criteria in choosing employees. If a job requires lifting 50-pound boxes, you may test applicants to determine whether they can lift those boxes. Similarly, you may continue to give typists typing tests to determine their abilities.

WHAT CONSTITUTES EMPLOYER DISCRIMINATION?

The ADA prohibits several specific forms of discrimination in dealing with job applicants and employees with disabilities. These include:

1. *Limiting, segregating, or classifying the disabled in a way that limits their opportunities or status.* Employers cannot make assumptions about what a class of individuals with disabilities can or cannot do. They cannot maintain separate lines of promotion for employees with disabilities or restrict employees with disabilities from performing certain tasks that are essential to their position.

Example _____

XYZ Corporation has a separate job category for janitors with developmental disabilities, a category with lower pay and no benefits or seniority rights, even though their duties are the same as other janitors. This policy violates Title I of the ADA. An employer cannot adopt different pay scales, benefits, or promotion opportunities for employees with disabilities.

Employment activities must take place in an integrated manner. This means that employees with disabilities must not be segregated into particular work areas. Amenities must also be integrated.

Example _____

If your company's existing coffee-break room is inaccessible to disabled employees, a comparable area should be made available. The alternative room does not have to be the same size as long as it is comparably equipped.

2.　*Entering into discriminatory third-party contracts.* Employers must keep employees with disabilities in mind when entering into any contractual relationship such as collective bargaining agreements with unions, employment agency referrals, contracts with hotels for company seminars, or contracts with consultants.

Example _____

You contract with a hotel to hold a conference for your employees. Under the ADA, you have an affirmative obligation to investigate the accessibility of that location, either by checking it out firsthand or asking a local disability group to do so. In any event, you can protect yourself by ensuring that the contract with the hotel specifies that all rooms used for the conference be accessible in accordance with ADA standards.

3.　*Denying health insurance coverage to an individual with a disability.* All people with disabilities are entitled to equal access to all fringe benefits the employer provides, including any health insurance coverage. Employers may not refuse a job to a person with disabilities just because the company's insurance plan does not cover a particular disability or because of an anticipated increase in insurance costs. Employers also may not deny health insurance coverage to an employee based on a disability.

However, the law does not require that all medical conditions be covered. An employer can still offer insurance policies that limit coverage for certain procedures or treatments, such as a limit on the number of X-rays, or noncoverage of experimental procedures. Employers may also continue to offer policies that contain exclusions for preexisting conditions and certain types of claims such as psychological counseling or alcoholism, even though such exclusions might adversely affect people with disabilities. Coverage cannot be denied for illnesses unrelated to the preexisting condition.

Example _____

A new employee who is diagnosed as having diabetes prior to the start of employment cannot be denied the same health insurance coverage given to other employees. However, if the plan denies coverage for preexisting medical problems, the new employee's medical expenses for diabetes are not covered. If the diabetic employee later has medical claims based upon cancer that was diagnosed *after* the beginning of employment, the cancer-related claims must be covered, assuming cancer is not excluded from coverage.

4.   *Discriminating against a qualified individual on the basis of that person's relationship or association with a disabled individual.* This provision extends beyond family associations.

Example _____

A qualified individual cannot be denied employment because a roommate has acquired immunodeficiency syndrome (AIDS) or a spouse has cancer.

5.   *Using tests that screen out people with disabilities.* Employers may administer only those tests that reflect essential job requirements and the applicant's skills rather than his or her impairments. Any selection criteria that automatically screen out people with disabilities are prohibited.

Example _____

Mr. Stutts, who is dyslexic, was denied the job of heavy equipment operator because he could not pass a written test used by the employer to enter a training program that is a prerequisite for the job. The question to be answered here is whether the written test for the training program is a necessary criterion for the job of a heavy equipment operator. If it is, the question becomes whether a reasonable accommodation such as an oral test or a reader could be provided to ensure that the test reflects his job skills rather than his impaired ability to read.

6.   *Upholding discriminatory employment standards.* Like Title VII of the Civil Rights Act of 1964, the ADA prohibits both intentional and unintentional discrimination. A seemingly benign practice that has a disparate impact on disabled employees, such as requiring all employees to have a valid driver's license, could be challenged under the ADA. Under the Equal Employment Opportunity Commission regulations, however, certain policies that are uniformly applied may not be challenged under the disparate impact theory.

Example ——————————————————————————————

Your company has a policy that employees are not eligible for a leave of absence during the first six months on the job. Although this policy may have a disparate impact on employees with disabilities, it cannot be challenged under the ADA.

7. *Failing to make reasonable accommodations.* Employers must act affirmatively to restructure their organization of work to expand opportunities to disabled applicants and employees. This involves making reasonable accommodations to the known physical or mental limitations of an otherwise qualified individual with a disability unless the accommodation would impose an undue hardship on the operation of the business. "Reasonable accommodation" is a central concept in the ADA that touches on provisions in every title. It is discussed at length in Chapter 6.

8. *Conducting discriminatory medical examinations or inquiries.* One of the most immediate changes that must be made to comply with the ADA is a revision in the procedures used in evaluating and hiring new employees. Figures 2.1 and 2.2 sumarize the types of inquiries that can be made at different junctures in the hiring process.

Medical examinations are not permitted at the preemployment phase in the hiring process. During this period, employers may not make *any* inquiries about disabilities, absenteeism, illness, or worker's compensation history. That includes job applications, interviews, and background or reference checks. You can ask questions relating to the applicant's ability to perform job-related functions, but you may not ask questions in terms of disability. Chapter 3 offers some ground rules for interviewing disabled job applicants.

Example ——————————————————————————————

In hiring drivers to deliver pizzas, an employer may ask whether an applicant has a driver's license but not whether the applicant has a visual disability.

The only legitimate purpose of a medical exam under the ADA is to determine if an applicant can perform specific job functions, not to determine if the person has a disability. After an offer of employment is made, employers may require a medical examination and condition their

Figure 2.1   Preemployment Tests at a Glance

Preoffer Qualification Test	Postoffer Medical Evaluation
Evaluates functional capacity to do the job.	Evaluates physical or mental health status.
Permitted prior to job offer.	Permitted only following offer. Employment may be contingent on passing.
Test must be job related.	Evaluation need not be job related. Mandatory postemployment evaluation must be job related and consistent with business necessity.
Exclusionary criteria must not tend to screen out individuals with disabilities unless job related and consistent with business necessity.	Exclusionary criteria must not tend to screen out individuals with disabilities unless job related and consistent with business necessity.
Assuming the above is true, an applicant may be denied a job based on failing a qualification test related to an essential job function only if the applicant cannot perform the essential job function or pass the qualification test with a reasonable accommodation.	Assuming the above is true, a job offer may be withdrawn based on evaluation results that indicate inability to meet employment criteria or if there is imminent risk of direct threat to self or others, based on current status.
Formal qualification tests must be the same for all. The employer may ask an applicant with a disability to describe or demonstrate the performance of a job function only if it appears that a known disability may interfere.	Medical tests and questions must be the same for all.
Actual decision whether or not to offer the job is employer's responsibility.	Actual decision whether or not to begin employment is employer's responsibility.

Source: Reprinted with permission from *The ADA: A Compliance Seminar* (manual). Long Grove, Ill.: Kemper Risk Management Services, 1992.

Figure 2.2   Medical Evaluation

The employer should provide the examining physician with:
- A functional job description.
- Job analysis indicating physical and mental stressors.
- A form to complete that summarizes the results of the medical evaluation.

The physician should provide the employer with:
- Results of the medical tests, including completed summary form.
- Clearance to perform specific job functions.
- Restrictions in performing specific job functions.
- Suggestions for accommodations.

Results of the medical evaluation:
- Final employment decision must be made by the employer.
- Medical records must be kept separate from personnel files.
- Medical records are strictly confidential, with the following exceptions:
  —Managers may be given information regarding restrictions and accommodations.
  —Safety/first-aid personnel may be given information relative to potential emergency treatment.
  —Government officials investigating compliance must be given relevant information on request.

Source: Reprinted with permission from *The ADA: A Compliance Seminar* (manual). Long Grove, Ill.: Kemper Risk Management Services, 1992.

offer on the results—as long as all new employees are required to take such an examination, regardless of disability. All medical records must be kept confidential.

Employee medical examinations: Once an individual is on the job, an employer cannot require a medical examination or inquire about an individual's disability unless it is job-related and consistent with business necessity.

Example _____

You notice that one of your employees has been losing her hair and looking tired, so you ask that she receive a medical exam for cancer within the next month. You are in violation of Title I of the ADA.

Example _____

Federal safety regulations require bus and truck drivers to have a medical examination at least biennially. The Occupational Safety and Health Administration (OSHA) lead standard requires that employees exposed to lead be tested periodically to determine the blood lead levels. These job-related medical tests are allowed under Title I.

Regarding drug testing, nothing in the ADA prohibits employers from testing applicants or employees for the presence of illegal drugs. Employers may refuse to hire an applicant or discipline an employee if tests detect illegal drug use. The term *illegal drugs* does not include drugs taken under medical supervision, even experimental drugs. An employer is not required to provide a rehabilitation program as a reasonable accommodation for a current drug user, but many companies have instituted employee assistance programs. They have found that it is more cost-effective to rehabilitate qualified employees than to terminate them. Whatever your decision, remember that *recovered* alcoholics and former drug addicts are protected by the act.

WHAT ARE YOUR DEFENSES?

Business Necessity

An employer may defend a practice that discriminates against a qualified individual with a disability if the practice is job related and consistent with business necessity.

Religious Organizations

Title I does not prohibit a religious corporation, educational institution, or society from giving preference in employment to individuals of a particular religion. This provision should be interpreted in a manner consistent with Title VII of the Civil Rights Act of 1964.

Example _____

A Mormon organization wishes to hire only Mormons to perform certain jobs. If a person with a disability applies for the job but is not a Mormon, the organization can refuse to hire the applicant. However, if two Mormons, one with a disability and one without a disability, apply for a job, the organization cannot discriminate against the applicant with a disability

Direct Threat to Health or Safety

Direct threat is defined as "a *significant* risk to the health or safety of others that cannot be eliminated with reasonable accommodation." Decisions in this regard cannot be based on generalizations or irrational fears about the disability. They must rest on the facts of the individual case. It is not the responsibility of applicants or employees to prove that they do not pose a risk in the workplace.

Example

In the case of the *School Board of Nassau County v. Arline*, it was found that Arline was qualified to be an elementary-school teacher even during the period when she had an active case of tuberculosis. The medical evidence showed that once a person with tuberculosis has begun antibiotic treatment, the chance of infecting others is quite low.[1]

Risk of Future Injury

If a worker's disability causes an accident on the job or a job-related illness, an employer's insurance coverage and worker's compensation costs could increase substantially. A customer or coworker who is injured as a result of an employee's disability could even bring a negligent hiring lawsuit against an employer who placed that person in a dangerous job without ensuring that he or she could do the work safely. On the other hand, denying employment to people with disabilities because they might cause accidents or have more frequent insurance claims is disability-based employment discrimination. The *School Board of Nassau County v. Arline* decision mentioned above clearly establishes that the employer's decision to deny a job to a person who may pose a risk of future injury must be based upon a reasonable medical judgment, not upon irrational fears. As with direct threats to health and safety, there must be not just an *elevated* risk of future injury but a *probability of substantial harm*.

---

[1]*School Board of Nassau County v. Arline*, 480 U.S. 273, 43 Fair Empl. Prac. Cas. 81 (1987).

Example _____

A railroad company's rules provided that any welder with epilepsy could not remain on the job. A worker who acquired epilepsy from an injury in an auto accident was discharged in accordance with company rules. The Supreme Court of Wisconsin held that the company rule was unreasonable because it was applied without first finding a reasonable probability of serious future harm. Medical testimony showed that the worker had never had an on-the-job seizure and had suffered no seizures since being placed on medication.

PRACTICAL TIPS FOR DEALING WITH RISK OF FUTURE INJURY

1. Don't make blanket rules that exclude all people with specific disabilities from certain jobs.
2. Examine the facts of each particular situation.
3. Be sure company physicians are informed of the law and understand that their personal medical opinion is less important than the generally accepted medical opinion.
4. Be sure that sound medical judgment proves that the individual's disability will create a substantial risk of serious injury or death in the job in question.
5. Be sure that all physicians analyzing an applicant's medical condition understand the exact physical duties of the job. If disputes arise with the applicant's personal physician, be sure the personal physician understands the job duties.
6. Encourage company physicians to consult with the applicant's personal physician and other doctors before making a final decision to disqualify a person because of a disability.
7. If an applicant is denied a job because of a disability, explain the problem to the applicant; if the applicant's physician has rendered a judgment of fitness for the job, also contact the physician to explain your decision.

Source: From pp. 122–123 of the *Employer's Guide to the Americans with Disabilities Act* by James G. Frierson. Copyright © 1992, by The Bureau of National Affairs, Inc., Washington, DC 20037. Reprinted with permission.

Food Service Workers

State and local public health departments are on the front lines of protecting the public health. These legitimate laws and regulations are not preempted by the ADA. The ADA requires the secretary of health and human services to use valid scientific evidence to determine which diseases are transmitted through the handling of food and then to issue an annually updated list of such diseases. The list includes common diseases such as hepatitis A, diseases caused by *Streptococcus* and *Salmonella* bacteria, as well as lesser known infections. AIDS and the human immunodeficiency virus are not included on the list.

If an individual has a communicable disease that can be transmitted through the handling of food, and if the risk of the disease's being transmitted on the job cannot be eliminated by reasonable accommodation, an employer may refuse to hire an individual in a food-handling job.

Example _____

John, a carpenter, has an infectious disease that can be eliminated by taking medication for a specified period of time. His employer must make the reasonable accommodation of allowing him time off to take the medication unless that would impose an undue hardship on the operation of the business.

What about AIDS?

Under the ADA, job applicants and employees with HIV, AIDS-related complex, or AIDS must be treated the same as other individuals with a disability. They cannot be excluded from food service jobs, health care jobs, or jobs that involve close contact with children.

SENSITIZING THE WORKPLACE

As a small business owner, you set the tone for your organization, and your attitudes are quickly reflected in your staff. You can foster a corporate culture of support for coworkers with disabilities by first confronting your own stereotypes. Following are common misconceptions about the disabled that can lead to unintentional discrimination.[2]

_____

[2]Michael Lotito et al., *Making the ADA Work for You*, 2d ed. (Northridge, Calif.: Milt Wright & Associates, 1992), 33–36.

•   *Certain jobs are more suited to people with disabilities.* People with disabilities are as diverse as any other group of workers. In the past, they were steered toward vocational choices to "fit" their disabilities, but this practice is unlawful under the ADA.

•   *Let's hire one to see what he or she can do.* A hiring decision should be based only on an objective evaluation of a person's competence to perform the essential functions of the job. You cannot use one person as a test case to generalize about the abilities of all disbled people.

•   *We need special training to work with the disabled.* Experience is helpful, but working with the disabled is essentially the same as working with any other group of people. Workers with disabilities want what anyone does: They want to show what they can accomplish; they want performance appraisals based on facts, not assumptions; they want control of their environment to the extent possible.

•   *Our insurance rates will be increased if we hire people with disabilities.* These fears are based on the false assumption that people with disabilities have higher accident and injury rates. Their rates are comparable to those of other employees. In the case of health coverage, the company's policy regarding coverage of preexisting conditions is still valid under the ADA.

•   *Accommodation is expensive.* The average accommodation costs far less than employers anticipate. The most common accommodation—adjustable scheduling—may cost little or nothing at all. For more information on costs for typical accommodations see Chapter 6.

•   *Persons with disabilities are better workers than able-bodied persons.* The danger in maintaining this stereotype is that it builds in higher expectations and standards for people with disabilities to satisfy. The average employee with disabilities is then viewed as a disappointment.

Attitudes don't change overnight, so you should start preparing your people *now*. Many training resources are available at little or no cost to help small businesses educate their staff about the requirements of the new law (see Resources). Besides posting notices as required by law,

Figure 2.3   Model Corporate Policy Statement Regarding Discrimination Against People with Disabilities

XYZ Corporation believes in equal employment opportunities for all individuals. The company is dedicated to ensuring that people with disabilities are not discriminated against in any aspect of employment, including hiring, recruitment, transfers, layoffs, terminations, compensation, education, training, and company-sponsored social activities.

This policy is intended to cover people who have a physical or mental impairment that substantially limits a major life activity, people who have a record of such impairments, or people regarded as having such impairments.

XYZ Corporation is also committed to making reasonable accommodations to qualified applicants and employees with disabilities that will enable them to perform the essential functions of a job. In this regard, reasonable accommodation procedures have been implemented to provide disabled people with a confidential means of requesting accommodations.

Employees are assured that they will be free from any reprisal or retaliation resulting from a request for accommodation and that all communications will be treated as confidential. Only those individuals involved in the request and those who may have relevant information will be contacted. The company may also contact outside organizations in an effort to investigate all aspects of a request for a reasonable accommodation.

The XYZ Corporation policy prohibiting discrimination against people with disabilities applies to all applicants and employees with disabilities as described above and protects employees at all job levels and positions. The [president, personnel department, etc.] is responsible for monitoring compliance with this policy and is available to answer questions about this policy or the Americans with Disabilities Act.

Figure 2.4   Sample CEO Cover Letter

I believe that equal employment is essential to the success of XYZ Corporation. It is our company policy, and my personal goal, that everyone in this company—job applicants and employees—be treated as an individual, without regard to arbitrary factors such as race, sex, or disability.

In July of this year a new law went into effect, the Americans with Disabilities Act, designed to give disabled Americans equal access to the mainstream of American life. The law guarantees, among other things, that qualified workers and job applicants will not be discriminated against on the basis of physical or mental disabilities.

In light of the new law, our company must:

1. Encourage individuals with physical or mental disabilities to apply for employment.
2. Take direct action to attract and hire qualified disabled employees.
3. Make sure that the workplace itself is accessible to all employees.
4. Make reasonable accommodations to help disabled employees perform the essential functions of their job.
5. Ensure that we respond to coworkers with disabilities in a sensitive and respectful manner.
6. Comply with all laws governing the employment of disabled people and cooperate with government agencies investigating complaints of discrimination against disabled people.
7. Emphasize the abilities of our employees rather than their disabilities or limitations.

This should be a companywide effort to comply with the spirit as well as the letter of the law. I want all employees at every level to join me in opening our workplace to all qualified people. I urge those of you who have a physical or mental condition that makes it difficult for you to do your job to identify yourself so that we can discuss what accommodations may be made to allow you to realize your full employment potential.

Our effort to hire and accommodate disabled workers is an investment in people that will help our company grow and prosper as we move into the twenty-first century. The U.S. Department of Labor predicts that there will be a shortage of qualified American workers by the year 2000. This means that businesses will have to actively recruit and train previously underutilized segments of the labor force, such as women, minorities, and the disabled. It is both an ethical and an economic imperative.

Signed _____
          Chief Executive Officer

Figure 2.5   Are You Discriminating Under Title I of the ADA?

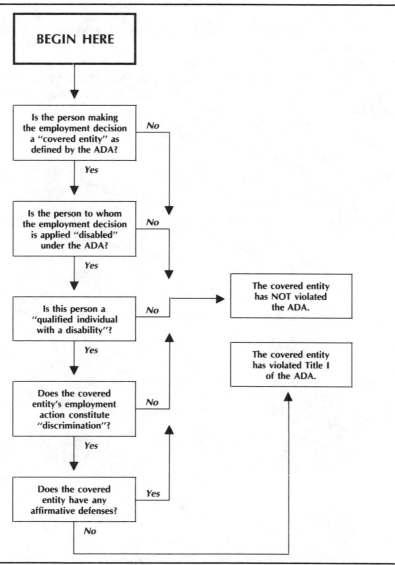

Source: Reprinted with permission from *Managing ADA: The Complete Compliance Guide,* by Robert Naeve and Ari Cowan. New York: John Wiley & Sons, 1992, pp. 3-5.

you can express your commitment to the ADA by developing a corporate policy on disabilities and holding a companywide meeting to discuss it. A sample policy and cover letter are shown in Figures 2.3 and 2.4.

The flowchart in Figure 2.5 summarizes the progression of questions to ask in assessing the legality of your hiring decisions under Title I of the ADA.

CHAPTER THREE

Interviewing Strategies

Although the Americans with Disabilities Act (ADA) doesn't prevent you from seeking the information you need to evaluate a job candidate, it does restrict the scope and purpose of your questioning. Many of the traditional questions that we take for granted on an application can no longer be asked.

Chapter 2 outlined the broad guidelines for preemployment tests and inquiries. In this chapter, we shall focus on the interviewing process to show you how to operate within the requirements of the law, how to put yourself and the applicant at ease, and how to get the information you need to make an appropriate hiring decision.

THE RIGHT WAY TO GAUGE A CANDIDATE'S SUITABILITY

The ADA categorically prohibits "fishing" for information about a candidate's physical or mental condition on an application form or during an interview. *You may inquire only about the person's ability to perform specific job-related functions.* For this reason, you must know the specific position the person is applying for and the essential functions of that position. (See Chapter 4 for more on identifying essential job functions.)

Examples _____

• It is a violation to ask, "Do you expect to need a lot of time off from work because of your condition?" You may, however, explain your company's attendance requirements or the unique requirements of the position in question and ask if the applicant can adhere to those standards.

• In interviewing a candidate for a maintenance position, you may not ask, "How did you lose your arm?" You may, however, ask the person to explain or demonstrate how he or she would use tools in that job.

Sometimes interviewers take the risk of asking illegal questions because they don't know how else to find out if a candidate can meet special job requirements such as overtime or weekend work. In his book *Swan's How to Pick the Right People Program*, William Swan, a nationally recognized expert on interviewing, points out a way that is both legal and sensitive. "The formula is simple," he says. "State the job requirement as clearly as you can and then ask the candidate a closed-ended question."[1]

For instance:

"This job will absolutely require you to be available for work on Saturdays . . ." (or *"to lift 50-pound boxes"* or *"to reach the top of a six-foot-high filing cabinet"* or *"to travel on short notice"*).

"If you can't meet this requirement you would be unable to function in this job. Therefore, let me ask you. . . ."

You have stated the job requirement as precisely as you could; now you ask a closed-ended question:

"Is there anything that would prevent you from meeting this essential requirement?"

Once you have become aware of a person's disability, you are obligated to provide a reasonable accommodation for that person to perform the essential functions of the job if the person is otherwise qualified.

You can become aware of a person's disability during an interview in one of three ways: (1) It is immediately apparent; (2) the person voluntarily brings it to your attention; (3) you ask a question about the person's ability to perform a function of the job that raises the issue of a need for an accommodation.

_____

[1] William Swan, *Swan's How to Pick the Right People Program* (New York: John Wiley & Sons, 1989), 268.

If the disability is evident or the person has brought it to your attention, you may ask how the person would do the job, with or without a reasonable accommodation.

If an applicant is blind, you could say, "The safety standards of this job require that the employee be aware of the chemicals that they are working with. How would you be aware of which chemicals you are handling? How might we accommodate you?"

In interviewing an applicant who is obviously deaf, you might say, "Attending and participating in daily meetings is an essential function of this job. How were you able to participate in meetings on your last job? What kind of accommodation do you suggest we provide?"

Interviewing is an art. The job interview is a notoriously stressful time for both parties. Each side is trying to make a good impression while forming judgments about the other. Some of the traditional barometers we rely on in evaluating applicants—subtle cues such as body language, communication style, and social skills—are not always reliable when dealing with people with disabilities. A firm handshake and upright posture can indicate confidence and respect, but don't make false assumptions based on a person's inability to communicate in the expected manner with his or her body. Look for character traits in other ways.

Interviewers need training in disability etiquette: How do you work with an interpreter? How do you shake hands with a blind person? Interviewers need to know when it is appropriate to discuss a disability and how to do so comfortably. The applicant will often assume that the interviewer's attitude reflects the company's philosophy about hiring people with disabilities. Some points to keep in mind when interviewing people with disabilities are listed on pages 37–38.

WHAT YOU CAN'T ASK

Asking an applicant the following kinds of questions would be a violation of the ADA:

- Have you ever been treated for the following listed conditions or diseases?
- List any conditions or diseases for which you have been treated in the past three years.
- Has anyone in your family ever had any of the following listed illnesses?
- Have you ever been hospitalized? For what?

- Have you ever been treated for a mental disorder?
- Have you ever been to a psychiatrist or psychologist? If so, for what?
- Have you ever been treated for drug addiction or alcoholism?
- Have you ever filed for worker's compensation benefits?
- How many times were you absent from your job because of illness?
- Are you taking any medication?
- Have you had a major illness in the last five years?
- Do you have any physical defects that preclude your performing certain tasks?
- Do you have any disabilities that would affect your performance in the position for which you are applying?
- Is there any health-related reason that would prevent you from doing the general type of work for which you are applying?
- How did your disability come about? What is the prognosis for recovery?

WHAT YOU CAN ASK

In general, you can ask questions related to essential job functions. If an applicant asks about an accommodation, you can ask what he or she will need to perform the job. You can also ask about the applicant's prior job responsibilities. Following are examples of specific questions that you are permitted to ask an applicant.

- Can you lift a 50-pound box?
- Can you stand [or sit] for an extended period of time?
- Can you be at work by 9:00 A.M. every day?
- Can you work five days a week?
- Can you reach the top of a six-foot-high filing cabinet?
- Do you have a driver's license?
- Can you perform the job for which you are applying either with or without an accommodation?
- What were your duties on your previous job and what accommodations were made to facilitate your work?
- Show me how you would perform a particular job task. (This question must be asked of everyone unless an applicant has a known disability that would seem to interfere with an essential job task.)

- If an applicant inquires about an accommodation, you can ask, what do you need to perform the job?

The ADA also allows the following actions:

- You can require postoffer medical examinations before an employee starts working and condition your offer on the results, provided that all entering employees in the same category are subjected to the same examination.
- You may require a preemployment drug test.
- You may refuse to hire an applicant with a disability if the individual poses a direct threat to himself or others.

Confidentiality

The ADA's confidentiality requirement concerning an individual's medical condition allows only three exceptions under which others may be told of a disability:

1. Supervisors and managers who need to know in order to make accommodations.
2. First aid and safety personnel.
3. Government officials investigating compliance with the ADA.

Employers may *not* inform coworkers or unions of accommodations that are made for a disabled employee. This restriction can be problematic in the case of a condition that is not readily apparent, such as cancer or a bad back. A coworker's knowledge of the disability could make him or her more cooperative in rearranging job schedules, trading nonessential job duties, and making other accommodations.

Even when accommodations don't directly involve other workers, they can appear unfair and lead to employee dissatisfaction, discrimination claims, and union grievances. Changing job duties, even nonessential ones, could violate the terms of a collective bargaining agreement, so proceed with caution. Any new collective bargaining agreements should provide for the right to make reasonable accommodations under the ADA. Remember, unions as well as employers are subject to the ADA.

Consistency

If several people in your organization participate in the hiring process, you must ensure that they are all following consistent, lawful practices.

All staff involved in hiring should be trained in ADA policies regarding interviewing, confidentiality, and reasonable accommodation. If possible, give one person with knowledge of employment law—yourself, perhaps—final review authority over all hiring decisions.[2]

WHO IS A JOB APPLICANT?

You can limit your liability under Equal Employment Opportunity Commission (EEOC) regulations by spelling out exactly who will be considered a job applicant. According to the Employer's Association in Charlotte, North Carolina, employers can do this by establishing a policy defining the conditions that a person must meet to be considered an applicant. If there is no such policy, then any person who calls about a job or sends in an unsolicited resumé can later claim that he or she was not hired for discriminatory reasons.

Even small business owners should consider incorporating the following points into a written job applicant policy:

- The policy should state that applications are accepted only when there is an open and listed job vacancy. If there are any exceptions to this provision, state them in the policy.
- State that every person must fill out an application form to be considered an applicant. This includes intercompany transfers.
- Applications should be accepted in person only.
- Regarding positions for which many resumés are submitted, set a cutoff number. For example, consider only the first 100 out of 1,000 resumés to be "applicants." Do not process the remaining 900.[3]

THE JOB APPLICATION

The questions you can and can't ask apply not only to face-to-face interviews but also to written job applications. The sample shown in

---

[2]Michael Lotito et al., *Making the ADA Work for You* (Northridge, Calif.: Milt Wright & Associates, 1992), 34.
[3]"Human Resource Measurements." *Personnel Journal* 71 (June 1992, special suppl.):3.

TIPS FOR INTERVIEWING PEOPLE WITH DISABILITIES

1. Introduce yourself. Identify who you are and what your job or role is.
2. Even if you are embarrassed about a person's disability, remember that the individual generally is not.
3. Maintain eye contact with the applicant. Avoid situations where you are standing over or looking down at the applicant. If the applicant uses a wheelchair, remain seated during the interview.
4. Do you shake hands with someone who has a prosthesis or limited use of his or her arms? Yes, if that is what you would usually do in this situation. If the person has quadriplegia, it's appropriate to touch him or her on the shoulder.
5. During an interview, sit as you do when interviewing other candidates. Some people conduct interviews from behind a desk, others choose to have none. Regardless of the person's disability, maintain the same level of attentiveness.
6. For people who are speech or hearing impaired, speak naturally; don't exaggerate your tone or lip movements. If you are asked to repeat a statement, don't say, "Never mind," or "it's not important."
7. Be patient in dealing with people who have difficulty speaking. In stressful situations, a person's speech often becomes even harder to understand. Don't finish a person's sentences or pretend to understand when you really do not. If you don't understand what has been said, ask the person to repeat it. If you are still unable to understand, look for alternative ways to communicate—perhaps by writing or through an interpreter.
8. When interviewing someone with a hearing impairment, a mental disability, or a learning disability, the usual, verbal method of presenting information may not be adequate. Be flexible and consider alternative methods of presentation. Try to determine whether the person understands what is being presented.
9. Give all applicants some kind of orientation during the interview—where they would work, what they would be doing, who they would interact with on the job.
10. Should you offer to help someone who has a disability? This is an individual decision. Usually, if people need help, they will ask for it. If you do offer and the person says yes, follow up by asking what you can do. Allow the person to hold onto you

rather than you holding him or her. Let the applicant control his or her own movements.

11. If a person indicates that he or she has a disability that makes it difficult to perform particular functions of the job, ask job-related follow-up questions.

12. Do not interact with a guide dog while the dog is working.

13. Long conversations can be very fatiguing to people who lip-read. Also, lip-reading is only 30 to 50 percent effective, and sometimes less. If an applicant lip-reads, speak in a normal way. Short sentences are best.

14. Maintain eye contact at all times with someone who is hearing impaired. If the person uses an interpreter, address the person, not the interpreter.

15. All wheelchairs are not the same size or shape. Just because one employee could access an area in a chair does not mean that everyone will be able to do so.

Source: Pimentel, Richard, et al., *What Managers and Supervisors Need to Know About the Americans with Disabilities Act*. Northridge, Calif.: Milt Wright & Associates, 1992, pp. 32, 48. Reprinted with permission.

Figure 3.1 meets the requirements of the ADA and other federal equal employment laws, as well as those of most state laws.

Question 12 on the sample application form can be adapted to fit the specific jobs offered by your company. The major functions of various jobs may be listed under Question 12 and individualized for each different job. Just be sure that all the questions you check involve a major duty of the position for which the person is applying. Question 12b, for example, asks if the applicant has a valid driver's license. This question should be checked only if the job involves driving.

APPLICATION FOR EMPLOYMENT

Acme Company
123 Elm Street
Anytown, Homestate 00000

Acme Company is an equal employment opportunity employer dedicated to a policy of nondiscrimination in employment upon any basis, including race, color, creed, religion, age, sex, national origin, ancestry, sexual orientation, marital status, military status, or the presence of any physical or mental medical condition or disability. In reading and answering the following questions, please keep in mind that none of the questions are intended to imply any limitations, illegal preferences, or discrimination based upon any non-job-related information.

This application will be given complete consideration, but its receipt does not imply that the applicant will be employed. Optional: Acme Company arranges for a surety bond for each employee, at the company's expense. Unless your background will pass scrutiny by a surety company (not related to the factors listed in the previous paragraph such as race or sex), it will be difficult or impossible to secure a surety bond, and the company will be unable to offer employment.

POSITION(S) APPLIED FOR: _____

Type of Work Desired: _____ Full Time _____ Part Time _____ Temporary

Date Available to Start Work: _____

PERSONAL DATA

Name _____ Social Security Number _____

Current Address: _____
               Street Address or Box Number   City   State   Zip

Permanent Address: _____
             (Leave Blank if the Same as Your Current Address)

Daytime Phone at Which You Can be Reached: (_____) _____
                                 Area Code

Evening Phone at Which You Can be Reached: (_____) _____
                                 Area Code

GENERAL INFORMATION

1. Have you ever applied for a job with this company in the past? ___ Yes ___ No
   If yes, please give the date of application and the position for
   which you applied. State your name at that time, if different from
   present name.

2. Have you ever been employed by this company in the past? ___ Yes ___ No
   If yes, please give dates of employment, position(s) held, and
   state your name while employed, if different from present name.

39

Figure 3.1 *(Continued)*

3. If hired, will you be able to work during the normal days and hours required for the position(s) for which you are applying?   ___ Yes   ___ No
   If no, please explain:

4. Do you have any commitments to another employer that might affect your employment with our company?   ___ Yes   ___ No
   If yes, please explain:

5. If hired, can you furnish proof that you are 18 years of age, or if under 18, do you have a permit to work?   ___ Yes   ___ No
   If no, please explain:

6. If hired, can you furnish proof that you are eligible to work in the United States? (If unsure of the documents needed to prove eligibility to work in the U.S., we will be happy to explain the legal requirements).   ___ Yes   ___ No
   If no, please explain:

7. Are you capable of satisfactorily performing the job(s) for which you are applying?   ___ Yes   ___ No
   If no, please explain:

8. Do you have any experience from your military service that would be relevant to the job(s) for which you are applying?   ___ Yes   ___ No
   If yes, please explain:

9. Do you have any language abilities (such as reading or speaking a foreign language) that might help you perform the job(s) for which you are applying?   ___ Yes   ___ No
   If yes, please explain:

10. Have you been convicted of a felony, or released from prison in the past 10 years? Note: A yes answer does not automatically disqualify you from employment since the nature of the offense, date, and type of job for which you are applying will be considered.   ___ Yes   ___ No
    If yes, please explain:

11. Are you charged with an unresolved criminal charge (have you been charged with a crime that has not yet resulted in a plea of guilty, court trial, or a dropping of the charge)? Note: A yes answer will not automatically disqualify you from employment.   ___ Yes   ___ No
    If yes, please explain fully:

Figure 3.1 *(Continued)*

12. Special Questions. Answer the questions in the following box <u>only if checked,</u> therefore indicating the question(s) are relevant to the job for which you are applying.

☐ a. Are you willing and physically able to travel to out-of-town locations, including overnight trips? If no, please explain: ___ Yes ___ No

☐ b. Do you have a valid driver's license? ___ Yes ___ No

☐ c. During the past seven years, have you ever been denied a driver's license, or convicted of a moving traffic offense, including, but not limited to, driving while intoxicated or reckless driving? If yes, please explain: ___ Yes ___ No

☐ d. Are you willing to undergo a physical examination by a physician, to prove you are physically able to perform the tasks of the job for which you have applied? ___ Yes ___ No

☐ e. Do you have all the licenses and professional certification listed in the job announcement, job advertisement, or job description, or that are necessary to perform the job(s) for which you are applying? If no, please explain: ___ Yes ___ No

☐ f. Do you know of any reasons that might make it difficult for the company to obtain a surety bond insuring your honesty? If yes, please explain: ___ Yes ___ No

☐ g. Example Skills Area Questions

Typing Speed (Corrected Words Per Minute) _____

Stenographic Speed (Words Per Minute) _____

Can you transcribe machine dictation? _____ Yes _____ No

List the business machines, computers, and word processors you can operate:

☐ h. Example Questions Where Job Involves Manual Labor (For purposes of illustration, assume the job requires lifting 50 lb. sacks)

Are you physically able to lift 50 lb. sacks on a continued, hour-by-hour, day-by-day basis? ___ Yes ___ No

If the answer to the preceding question is Yes, do you agree to take a test, at your own risk of injury, to prove your ability? And do you agree that the test will be conducted without any legal liability upon the company for any injuries which might result? ___ Yes ___ No

☐ i. Example Question Where the Job Involves Extra Trust (bank teller, bellboy, etc.)

Have you ever been convicted, pled guilty, or pled "no contest" to any criminal offense involving dishonesty or a breach of trust, including, but not limited to, theft, fraud, passing bad checks, credit card fraud, forgery, or other crime? If you were charged, but the charges were dropped or you were acquitted, answer "No." Note: A yes answer does not automatically disqualify you from employment since the nature of the offense and date will be considered. If yes, please explain: ___ Yes ___ No

Figure 3.1 *(Continued)*

13. EMPLOYMENT HISTORY

PRESENT & FORMER EMPLOYERS
(List Most Recent First)   MAY WE CONTACT YOUR PRESENT EMPLOYER? _____ Yes _____ No

Company Name	Job Title & Duties
Address	
	Dates of Employment From To
City, State, Zip	Reason for Leaving
Supervisor (and phone number, if known)	Your Name When Employed. If Different From Present Name

Company Name	Job Title & Duties
Address	
	Dates of Employment From To
City, State, Zip	Reason for Leaving
Supervisor (and phone number, if known)	Your Name When Employed. If Different From Present Name

Company Name	Job Title & Duties
Address	
	Dates of Employment From To
City, State, Zip	Reason for Leaving
Supervisor (and phone number, if known)	Your Name When Employed. If Different From Present Name

Company Name	Job Title & Duties
Address	
	Dates of Employment From To
City, State, Zip	Reason for Leaving
Supervisor (and phone number, if known)	Your Name When Employed. If Different From Present Name

Figure 3.1 *(Continued)*

Company Name	Job Title & Duties
Address	
	Dates of Employment From To
City, State, Zip	Reason for Leaving
Supervisor (and phone number, if known)	Your Name When Employed. If Different From Present Name

Please Account for Any Time You Were Not Employed After Leaving School in the Past Ten Years
(You need not list any unemployment periods of one month or less)

Time Period(s)   Reason(s) for Unemployment

_____

_____

_____

IF YOU WERE UNABLE TO LIST ALL PAST JOBS OR PERIODS OF UNEMPLOYMENT ON THIS FORM,
PLEASE ATTACH ADDITIONAL INFORMATION ON A BLANK SHEET OF PAPER.

14. EDUCATIONAL DATA

SCHOOLS ATTENDED	NAME OF SCHOOL AND LOCATION	DID YOU GRADUATE? YES NO	DEGREE/ DIPLOMA/ CERTIFICATE?	GRADE POINT AVERAGE	MAJOR COURSE OF STUDY
HIGH SCHOOL	_____ CIRCLE HIGHEST GRADE COMPLETED 1 2 3 4 5 6 7 8 9 10 11 12		DO NOT ANSWER		DO NOT ANSWER
TECHNICAL, VOCATIONAL, BUSINESS OR MILITARY TRAINING					
COLLEGE OR UNIVERSITY					
GRADUATE SCHOOL					
PROFESSIONAL SEMINARS					

ADDITIONAL JOB-RELATED SEMINARS, SHORT COURSES, WORKSHOPS, OR OTHER EDUCATIONAL EXPERIENCES:

Figure 3.1 *(Continued)*

15. REFERENCES: LIST THREE INDIVIDUALS WHO ARE NOT FORMER EMPLOYEES OR RELATIVES

NAME	ADDRESS	CITY, STATE, ZIP	PHONE NUMBER	OCCUPATION

16. OTHER JOB-RELATED EXPERIENCE. Some people gain job-related experience in positions other than as an employee. For instance, an accountant may gain experience as a treasurer of a civic or school organization, or a manager may gain experience while working on civic projects, or in school organizations, or in PTA activities. Please list and describe any paid or unpaid activities, honors, experience, or training that might aid you in performing the job(s) for which you have applied, and have not been listed previously in this application. (You may omit any activities, honors, memberships or other items that tend to identify your race, sex, national origin, age, disability or other personal traits that you prefer not to disclose.)

17. Please add any additional information (except that which identifies your race, sex, age, religion, national origin, disability or other non-job-related personal information) that you think may be relevant to a decision to hire you.

Figure 3.1 *(Continued)*

IMPORTANT

Please Read Carefully and Initial Each Paragraph Before Signing

By my signature and initials placed below, I promise that the information provided in this employment application (and accompanying resume, if any) is true and complete, and I understand that any false information or significant omissions may disqualify me from further consideration for employment, and may be justification for my dismissal from employment, if discovered at a later date. I agree to immediately notify the company if I should be convicted of a felony, or any crime involving dishonesty or a breach of trust while my job application is pending, or during my period of employment, if hired.

_____ Initials

I authorize the investigation of all statements contained in this application (and accompanying resume, if any). I also authorize the company to contact my present employer (unless otherwise noted in this application form), past employers, and listed references. I understand that the company may request an investigative consumer report from a consumer reporting agency that includes information as to my character, general reputation, personal characteristics, and mode of living. I understand that the investigative consumer report may involve personal interviews with my neighbors, friends, relatives, former employers, schools, and others. I also understand that under the Federal Fair Credit Reporting Act I have the right to make a written request to the company, within a reasonable time, for the disclosure of the name and address of the consumer reporting agency so that I may obtain a complete disclosure of the nature and scope of the investigation.

_____ Initials

I authorize any person, school, current employer (except as previously noted), past employer(s), and organizations named in this application form (and accompanying resume, if any) to provide the company with relevant information and opinion that may be useful to the company in making a hiring decision, and I release such persons and organizations from any legal liability in making such statements.

_____ Initials

I give permission for a complete physical examination, including a drug screening exam and X-rays, and I consent to the release to the company of any and all medical information, as may be deemed necessary by the company in judging my capability to do the work for which I am applying.

_____ Initials

I understand that if my employment is terminated by the company for dishonesty, breach of trust, or any criminal acts the authorities may be notified and I may be criminally prosecuted. I also understand that, if hired, I may not hold other employment, nor engage in sales, investments or other activities that create a conflict of interest with my position with this company.

_____ Initials

I understand that this application does not, by itself, create a contract of employment. I understand and agree that, if hired, MY EMPLOYMENT IS FOR NO DEFINITE PERIOD OF TIME, and may, regardless of the date of payment of my wages or salary, BE TERMINATED AT ANY TIME. I understand that NO PERSON IS AUTHORIZED TO CHANGE ANY OF THE TERMS MENTIONED IN THIS EMPLOYMENT APPLICATION FORM.

_____ Initials

Date _____   Signed: _____

THIS APPLICATION FOR EMPLOYMENT WILL REMAIN ACTIVE FOR _____ WEEKS.

Source: From pp. 183–189 of the *Employer's Guide to the Americans with Disabilities Act* by James G. Frierson. Copyright © 1992, by The Bureau of National Affairs, Inc., Washington, DC 20037. Reprinted with permission.

Companies that give entering employees a medical or physical examination can add the following statement just before the signature line on the job application form:

If you are hired, a medical examination will be required before you start work. If the examination discloses medical conditions that prevent you from successfully performing the essential functions of the job, the company will attempt to make accommodations to allow you to work. If no reasonable accommodations can be found, or they cause an undue hardship on the company, the tentative offer of employment will be withdrawn.[4]

RECRUITING DISABLED WORKERS

As competition for qualified labor becomes more intense, companies will have to expand their outreach efforts into new areas. Many companies today have proactive disability recruitment programs as part of their commitment to business growth and economic development within their communities.

Consider contacting the following sources in recruiting disabled applicants:

- College placement offices.
- Community social service organizations.
- Local chapters of disability organizations such as the American Cancer Society or the American Diabetes Association.
- State vocational rehabilitation agencies.

Don't overlook your own organization in recruiting applicants. Current employees who may become disabled on the job can provide you with a pool of qualified applicants if your company is committed to retaining them through effective disabilities management. This is one reason why many employers today have established liberal disability benefits, disability leaves, retraining programs, and return-to-work programs for employees who become disabled.

---

[4]From p. 192 of the *Employer's Guide to the Americans with Disabilities Act* by James G. Frierson. Copyright © 1992, by The Bureau of National Affairs, Inc., Washington, DC 20037. Reprinted with permission.

Figure 3.2   Sample Job Advertisements

Discriminatory	Nondiscriminatory
Perfect job for attractive young woman with lots of personality.	ABC Co. seeks receptionist with 2–3 yrs. experience.
Looking for high school grad with good typing skills.	Must be multitask oriented—able to handle calls and incoming visitors.
Must be under 40 with valid driver's license.	Must type 45 wpm and be familiar with ATT Centrex phone features.
Apply in person at: 208 Garland Drive Culver City, CA.	Professional demeanor is important.
	Applications accepted from 9–10 A.M., Mon–Fri; or call 310-000-0000; or send resume to: 208 Garland Dr., Culver City, CA. Attn: Mr. Bristow, Personnel Manager.
	Equal Opportunity Employer. Women, minorities & disabled people encouraged to apply.

Guidelines for Preparing Job Advertisements

Job announcements should not include language that screens out people with disabilities. They should give a positive indication that disabled applicants will be considered for employment in a nondiscriminatory manner. All recruitment notices should include information on the essential functions of the job. This will attract people with appropriate qualifications, including those with disabilities. If possible, give applicants an option of contacting the company by phone or mail so that people with mobility impairments can have equal access to the opportunity. Many job announcements indicate that the employer does not discriminate on the basis of age, sex, religion, race, national origin, or disability. (See Figure 3.2.)

CHAPTER FOUR

Identifying Essential Job Functions

The Americans with Disabilities Act (ADA) is designed to ensure that *qualified* individuals with disabilities are not discriminated against in hiring and employment. An individual is qualified if he or she can perform, with or without reasonable accommodation, the essential functions of the position. Under this provision, the decision as to whether or not an individual is qualified hinges on determining which functions are essential. It's basically a two-step process: first, you determine if the individual is "otherwise qualified" for the position; then you pinpoint the fundamental duties of the position.

THE "OTHERWISE QUALIFIED" ANALYSIS

An individual is "otherwise qualified" for a position if he or she satisfied the prerequisites for the position. Job-related qualification standards may include:

- Education
- Experience
- Skills
- License
- Training

- The ability to meet regular attendance requirements for the position
- The ability to perform essential functions without posing a "direct threat" to oneself or others
- The ability to adhere to all personnel policies

The determination of an individual's ability to perform essential functions must be based on the person's capabilities at the time of employment. It should not be based on speculation about the employee's future ability or on concerns about increased health insurance premiums or worker's compensation costs.

THE ESSENTIAL FUNCTIONS ANALYSIS

We have seen in preceding chapters that the questions we ask in a job interview, the tests we administer to applicants, and the screening criteria we apply must all center on essential job functions. This is a key concept in the ADA, yet the law itself does not offer a precise definition of "essential."

Under the implementating regulations of the Equal Employment Opportunity Commission (EEOC), the term *essential functions* means job duties that are fundamental to the position, not marginal. A job function may be considered essential for any of several reasons:

- *The position exists to perform that function.* If an individual is hired to proofread documents, the ability to proofread would then be an essential function because it is the only reason the position exists.

- *There are a limited number of employees among whom that function can be distributed.* If an employer has only a few available employees for the volume of work to be done, it may be necessary for each employee to perform several functions. In this situation, functions that might not be essential if there were a larger staff may become essential because the staff size is small in relation to the volume of work. For instance, because there are more people on a day shift in a hospital, a function that may be nonessential during the first shift could be critical for a person on the second shift.

- *The function is highly specialized.* In some highly skilled positions, employees are often hired for their expertise or ability to perform a particular function. Even if the function is not performed regularly, it may be considered essential to the job.

The process of analyzing essential job functions is mapped out in the flowchart in Figure 4.1. It is basically a two-step process.

Step 1: Begin by asking yourself why the position exists and what it is that you are actually paying the person to do. Break the position down into individual tasks. As you look at each task, ask yourself whether it is a basic, necessary, and integral part of the job (an "essential function") or a peripheral, incidental, or minimal part of the job (a "marginal function"). Get input from other people who are currently doing the job or have done it in the past.

Step 2: Next, examine the effect of removing the function from the position. Ask yourself, If the function is removed, will the basic purpose of the job be altered or will there be only an occasional inconvenience?

Example _____

A person with epilepsy applied for the job of group counselor at a juvenile hall. The employer withdrew his initial job offer when it was learned that the applicant did not have a driver's license. Driving was required for emergencies and to transport juveniles to court appearances. While it was necessary for some counselors to be available to drive, it was not essential that they *all* be available.

In determining whether or not a function is essential, the EEOC will consider the following types of evidence:

• The employer's judgment.

• Written job descriptions prepared before advertising the job or interviewing applicants.

• The amount of time spent on the job performing the function. Although there is no specific percentage requirement, if an individual rarely performed the function, that would be relevant to the analysis.

• The consequences of not requiring the incumbent to perform the function. For instance, although a firefighter might not often have to carry people down a ladder, failure to perform this task when necessary could have serious consequences.

Figure 4.1   Process for Analyzing the Essential Functions of a Job

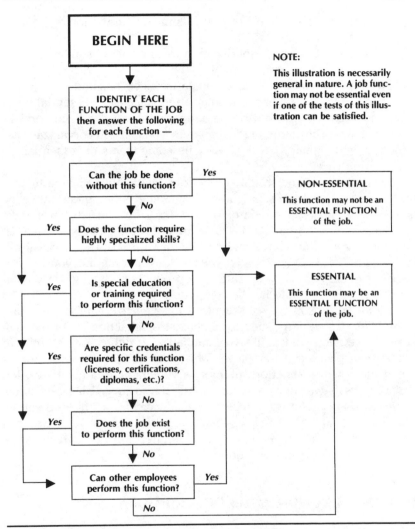

Source: Reprinted with permission from *Managing ADA: The Complete Compliance Guide*, by Robert Naeve and Ari Cowan. New York: John Wiley & Sons, 1992, pp. 3-22.

- The terms of a collective bargaining agreement.

- The work experience of past incumbents in the job.

- The current work experience of incumbents in similar jobs.

This list is not all-inclusive. For instance, decisions under the Rehabilitation Act have established regular attendance as an essential function, and there is little reason to suppose this rule will not prevail under the ADA. The nature of the employer's business, its organizational structure, and similar factors all may be components of "essentiality" in any given case.[1]

Remember that the essential functions test is not designed to second-guess an employer's judgments regarding either quantitative or qualitative production standards or to force employers to lower their standards. You are free to set your standards as high as you wish, as long as they are job related and consistent with business necessity. If you require typists to accurately type 65 words per minute, you will not have to explain why an inaccurate work product or a typing speed of 50 words per minute would not be adequate.

Although the ADA does not require employers to create and maintain written job descriptions, successful defense of an action under the ADA could hinge upon your ability to establish what duties are essential to a particular position. An employer who relies on subjective judgments about the essential functions of a job is vulnerable to a challenge. Job descriptions that are accurately prepared prior to advertising, recruiting, or interviewing applicants will be solid evidence of a position's essential functions. It is important to keep the descriptions current. A job description is useless—in fact, potentially dangerous—if it misrepresents the actual requirements of a position.[2]

WRITING FUNCTIONAL JOB DESCRIPTIONS

If a complex set of job descriptions is not available or desirable, you may wish to perform a job analysis at the time the vacancy occurs. You

---

[1]Zachary Fasman, *What Business Must Know about the ADA* (Washington, DC: U.S. Chamber of Commerce, 1992), 15.
[2]Michael Lotito et al., *Making the ADA Work for You,* 2d ed. (Northridge, Calif.: Milt Wright & Associates, 1992), 32.

could ask an incumbent employee to describe his or her job in detail, specifying what tasks are performed, how much time is spent on each, and whether some of the duties could be performed by other workers. This information could provide the basis for a clear and accurate description of job duties.

Here are some other guidelines to follow in deciding what functions of a job are essential:

• Document all important job functions. A preexisting document avoids the appearance that an employer is rationalizing the rejection of an individual with a disability.

• Be accurate and realistic. Job descriptions should describe the actual duties of the position rather than an ideal candidate.

• Stay current. Some jobs change rapidly. Outdated or inaccurate job descriptions can hurt an employer, so rescind all current job descriptions pending a review.

• Be flexible. In describing the essential functions of a job, don't take the attitude that "this is the way it has always been done." Employers who can pare their jobs down to core elements are more likely to prevail in litigation.

• Review job descriptions with employees. It is always a good idea for employees to understand exactly what is expected of them. Solicit their input in developing functional job descriptions and document their acceptance of the descriptions.

• Consider the total work environment.

• Avoid vague or ambiguous expressions such as "other duties as assigned." If included, these items should be listed separately as nonessential functions.[3]

Employers often include tasks in job descriptions that are incidental to the job. A common example is the requirement that applicants possess a driver's license for nondriving jobs. The employer may believe that someone who drives will be on time for work, work more overtime,

---

[3]Fasman, *What Business Must Know about the ADA*, 16.

or be able to do occasional errands. The essential functions requirement assures that a person who cannot drive because of a disability is not disqualified if he or she can do the fundamental duties of the job.

It is important to review the job duties not in isolation but in the context of the actual work environment. In *Hall v. United States Postal Service*, a case brought under the Rehabilitation Act of 1973, a postal employee won the right to a trial on the question of whether the ability to lift a 70-pound sack was an essential requirement of a postal clerk's job. The applicant maintained that in her prior work as a postal clerk she had never seen any clerks doing heavy lifting, nor had she done any herself. The applicant and the employer also disagreed on whether the employee's previous job was the same as the one for which she now was applying. Thus, whether the employee's observations and experience established the essentiality of the lifting requirement depended to some extent on whether she previously had worked in the same job.[4]

In addition, the essential function requirement focuses on the desired result rather than on the means of accomplishing it.

Example

In a job requiring the use of a computer, the essential function is the ability to access, input, and retrieve information from the computer. It is not essential that the person be able to use the keyboard or visually read the computer screen if adaptive equipment or software would enable the person with the disability—a visual impairment or limited hand control, for instance—to control the computer and access the information. The relevant question would be whether the acquisition of the equipment would be a reasonable accommodation, given the factors to be considered in making that determination.

Although employees and applicants may challenge the employer's determination of what is an essential function, the law makes it clear that the employer's judgment will be a factor.

Figure 4.2 outlines the steps to take in developing a functional job description.

---

[4]Henry H. Perritt, Jr., *The Americans with Disabilities Act Handbook*, 2d ed. (New York: John Wiley & Sons, 1991), 60.

Figure 4.2 Steps in Developing a Functional Job Description

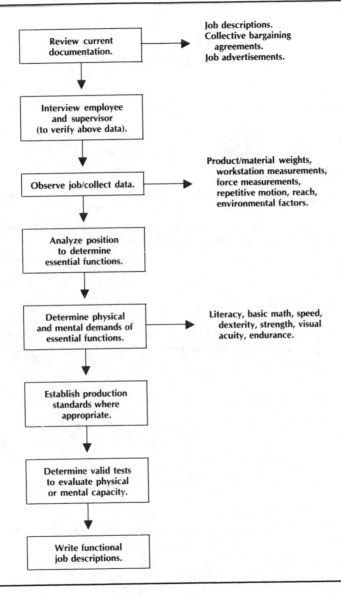

Figure 4.3   Suggested Format for a Functional Job Description

Job Title:

Ensure that the job name is consistent on all related documents, including advertisements, collective-bargaining documents, and internal job postings.

Department:

Status:

Exempt or nonexempt.

Principal Objective of Position:

This should be a brief one- or two-sentence statement of the overall function of the job—i.e., why the job exists.

Reporting Relationships:

Qualifications:

This includes education, certification, licensure, experience, and special skills (e.g., "must be able to program in RBase"; "must be able to type 75 words per minute").

Attendance Requirements:

Time: Note hours per week and time of beginning and end of shift. Include any rotation scheme or exceptions. For example, if 10-hour shifts are required periodically, note this.

Days per week: Note regular days and exceptions. If six-day workweeks are required periodically, note this.

Minimum acceptable attendance: Reference your company's sick-day and vacation-day policies and note minimum attendance requirements.

Quality Standards:

Note required quality standards and time by which employee must be able to meet those standards. If challenged, you must be able to show how and when quality is evaluated and that the same standards are expected of current employees.

Figure 4.3   *(Continued)*

Quantity Standards:

Maximum production rate (if machine paced): Note the maximum machine rate the employee is required to maintain. If challenged, you must be able to show that all current employees can keep up with this pace and that this ability is essential. Include seasonal fluctuations, if relevant.

Average production rate (if machine paced): Note the average rate at which the machine runs. If challenged, you must be able to show that all current employees must be able to keep up with this rate.

Minimum acceptable production rate (if employee paced): Note minimum acceptable standards required of employees to perform this job. It is often expected that new employees will not immediately be able to meet this standard; if this is the case, note by when standards must be met.

Work Environment:

Temperature: Note temperature extremes. This is especially relevant if an employee works in an environment that is not temperature controlled, or if controlled temperatures are out of the normal comfort zone (for example, a freezer area).

Lighting: Note lighting extremes, especially if lighting is dim or shadowed.

Personal Protective Equipment:

Note any safety equipment or clothing required, including gloves, hearing protection, respirators, thermal wear.

Essential Functions:

List all basic tasks required to perform the job. Wording should be in terms of *what* is required, not *how* it is done. For example, say "move the box," rather than "lift the box." It is usually best to list job functions in order of their occurrence.

Other Job Duties:

List marginal or occasional tasks that might have to be completed on an as-needed basis.

Source: Reprinted with permission from *The ADA: A Compliance Seminar* (manual). Long Grove, Ill.: Kemper Risk Management Services, 1992.

Figure 4.4 Sample Position Description

Job Title: Word Processor
Department: Marketing
Status: Nonexempt

Principal Objective of Position: To type a variety of documents at acceptable levels of accuracy and within specified deadlines.

Reporting Relationships: Reports to Word Processing Supervisor. Interfaces with personnel from all departments.

Qualifications:
High school diploma or equivalent.
Must be able to type 75 words per minute.
One year experience as Clerk/Word Processor or equivalent experience.
Experience with WordPerfect or equivalent word processing software.
Must be able to use a LAN system.
Dictaphone experience essential.
Must demonstrate good spelling and grammatical skills.
Must be able to read proofreading symbols.

Attendance Requirements: Normal work hours are 9 A.M. to 5 P.M., Monday through Friday. Position requires some weekend work during peak season, from June to September.

Quality/Quantity Standard: Employee must be able to process a minimum of 25 pages per day. Final copy must be free of typographical and formatting errors.

Essential Functions:
1. Types letters, memos, reports, contracts, proposals, service directives, statistical tables, and similar items from hard copy or dictaphone using automated systems. Sets up document format and layout. Corrects spelling and punctuation errors.
   - Inputs data onto macros at direction of supervisor.
   - Uses basic and special functions for automated systems to input data.
   - Sends documents to printers according to established procedures.
2. Proofreads work for accuracy.
3. Designs, types, formats, and binds manuals. Performs cutting and pasting activities.
4. Operates photocopier and binding machines.
5. Operates acetate machine to prepare overhead transparencies.

Other Duties:
1. Provides clerical support to technical staff as needed.
2. Distributes letters, reports, memos, and other documents.

KEY ELEMENTS IN A FUNCTIONAL JOB DESCRIPTION

Job descriptions should have separate sections that cover:

- Qualification standards (e.g., education, experience, skills, licenses, training).
- Essential functions of the position.
- Nonessential (desirable) functions of the position.

A suggested format for a functional job description is shown in Figure 4.3. Figure 4.4 illustrates how to apply that format to a particular position—in this case, a beginning word-processing job.

JOB RESTRUCTURING

Is an employer obligated to reorganize the work to eliminate a job requirement that cannot be met because of an employee's handicap? The answer in many cases is yes.

Job restructuring is one of the many forms of reasonable accommodation that will be discussed at length in Chapter 6. This could involve redelegating certain assignments, exchanging assignments with another employee, redesigning procedures for accomplishing certain tasks, or implementing modified work schedules. Using the example of the juvenile counselor with epilepsy mentioned earlier, you could redistribute all transporting responsibilities to the other three workers.

The burden of justifying the organization of work rests with the employer. It involves analyzing how jobs are defined and how tasks are allocated among jobs. You can justify a refusal to accommodate only by establishing that the accommodation would either eliminate an essential function of the job or would impose an undue hardship. A well-thought-out job description could be critical in an essential functions defense.

CHAPTER FIVE

Enforcement of ADA Employment Regulations

REMEDIES

The remedies and procedures provided by Title I of the Americans with Disabilities Act (ADA) are the same as those available under Title VII of the Civil Rights Act of 1964 to persons discriminated against on the basis of race, color, religion, sex, or national origin. These remedies include:

- Hiring or reinstatement
- Promotion
- Increase in wages or benefits
- Back pay, front pay, and other wage adjustments
- Adjustments in policies and procedures
- Monetary awards and fines, including payment of attorney's fees, expert witness fees, and court costs
- Increased reporting requirements
- Oversight and monitoring of employment practices
- Prevention of retaliation
- Other administrative and civil remedies

Damage awards are capped at $50,000 against firms with 15 to 100 employees and at $300,000 for larger firms. The caps are the same as those in Title VII of the Civil Rights Act, and Congress is considering removing them soon.

A violation of Title VII can be established in one of two ways: by proving intentional discrimination or by proving that a particular employer policy has a disparate impact on a defined group. A plaintiff cannot build a disparate impact case based on *general* employment practices.

Because the ADA adopts all of Title VII's remedial provisions, any amendments to Title VII are fully applicable to the ADA. For instance, the ADA is silent about the right to a jury trial, but the Civil Rights Reform Act of 1990 amended Title VII and afforded juries in cases alleging intentional discrimination and seeking compensatory or punitive damages. This provision will apply to the ADA as well.

A plaintiff who lodges a disability-related discrimination charge cannot bypass the administrative remedies of Title VII and go directly to court under Title I of the ADA. The person must follow the same procedures and secure the same remedies as women and minorities do under Title VII. Nevertheless, the ADA does not limit the person's access to the rights, remedies, and procedures of other federal and state laws.

The ADA encourages the informal resolution of claims through settlement negotiations, conciliation, facilitation, mediation, fact-finding, minitrials, and arbitration. However, the use of alternative methods is voluntary and doesn't prevent a person from pursuing the remedies provided for in the ADA without having exhausted the informal procedures.

What actually happens when an employee files a Title VII discrimination complaint? Let's follow the process step by step.

ENFORCEMENT—THE ROLE OF THE EEOC AND STATE AGENCIES

Responsibility for enforcing Title I of the ADA rests with the federal Equal Employment Opportunity Commission (EEOC), the administrative agency that enforces almost all major federal employment legislation.

In addition to the federal laws, most states have enacted their own fair employment laws and have created state equal employment opportunity (EEO) agencies to enforce them. Of the 50 states, 42 have state EEO agencies. When a complaint is filed with the EEOC, that agency will defer the complaint to the state agency if one exists. Practically speaking, most federal EEO complaints are investigated and resolved not by the EEOC but by state EEO agencies.

Charges must be filed with the EEOC within 180 days of the alleged discriminatory act, or within 300 days in deferral states with approved enforcement agencies. This is the statute of limitations for Title VII actions under federal law. An untimely charge must be dismissed no matter how strong the employee's case.

Procedurally, Title VII of the 1964 Civil Rights Act is one of the more complicated statutes on the books. Under most federal laws, such as the Bankruptcy Act, for instance, a plaintiff may go directly into federal court. A Title VII plaintiff must first file a complaint with his or her state EEO agency. That agency then has exclusive jurisdiction over the complaint for 60 days. This legal requirement is based on the theory that the state agency should be given the first opportunity to resolve the complaint, thus eliminating the need for involvement on a federal level. Most state EEO agencies have ongoing contracts with the EEOC under which they are paid for each EEOC-deferred complaint they handle. Although the EEOC has the right to take back a deferred complaint after 60 days, it generally allows the state agency to take as much time as it needs to reach a resolution. The EEOC usually adopts the determination of the state EEO agency as its own decision. Only in rare cases will an employee convince the EEOC to look at a complaint that was dismissed by the state EEO agency for lack of probable cause.

After a complaint has been filed with the state EEO agency, the agency will begin an investigation and will send a copy of the complaint to the employer along with an investigatory questionnaire.

When you receive the complaint, check to see which state or federal statutes are being relied on. If you are located in a deferral state, examine the charge to determine whether the employee has filed charges under both federal and state law. Sometimes an employee files charges under either federal or state law and improperly assumes that he or she has filed charges under both. Failure to file under both federal and state law is significant to you as an employer because the laws may have different statutes of limitations, they may cover different defined groups of employees, or they may provide for different remedies. Even though most federal EEOC complaints are deferred to state EEO agencies, that does not mean that the complaint has been filed under state law.

The consequence to an employee who mistakenly assumes that he or she has also filed under state law is that the statute of limitations under the state law may expire. In fact, it sometimes happens that the statute of limitations expires on a state cause of action at the same time that the state EEO agency is in the process of investigating a deferred federal complaint.

PRIVATE SETTLEMENT WITH THE COMPLAINANT

In the face of an enormous caseload, EEO agencies encourage early settlement between employer and employee. While your initial response to a discrimination complaint might be one of indignation, in many cases it is in your interests in the long run to reach an early settlement. Early settlement is generally less expensive than a later settlement, and it is certainly less expensive than losing an EEO lawsuit. Settlement prior to agency investigation avoids exposing the company to state and federal probes. Although settlement is possible at any stage in the process, it is only at this early stage that it can be negotiated in the context of "no probable cause." As we shall see later, a settlement after the investigation has been completed is framed in the context of a conciliation agreement, which recites the fact that the investigation disclosed probable cause to support the allegation of unlawful discrimination. The EEOC and its agencies maintain an index of respondents, including prior findings of probable cause, so it is probably best to eliminate this possibility.

Settlement prior to the investigation is effected by the employer communicating directly with the complainant. The agency need not be involved in this process. The settlement is put in writing, and the employee is obligated to withdraw the complaint. EEOC and state agencies require that the complainant formally request to withdraw the complaint.

THE INVESTIGATORY QUESTIONNAIRE

If you decide not to settle with the employee at this point, you will have to complete the investigatory questionnaire within a certain amount of time specified in the questionnaire. The time and effort put into completing the questionnaire are well spent. Your responses will commit you to a specific line of defense that you will have to maintain throughout the case. Strong responses could even eliminate the need for a sit-down conference and end the matter with a finding of "no probable cause." Don't hesitate to ask for additional time to respond to the questionnaire. Such requests are routinely granted.

In completing the questionnaire, begin by conducting your own investigation into the complaint. Do not automatically dismiss the allegations without looking into them personally. While you would of course prefer to believe that your supervisors and other employees acted in accordance with the law, it is better for *you* to uncover any illegal actions by employees before they are uncovered by the EEO. If conducted properly, an in-house investigation will uncover critical strengths and weaknesses in your position and will assist in preparing a specific response to the questionnaire. Figure 5.1 is a sample investigatory questionnaire from the New York State Division of Human Rights.

If your in-house investigation finds that the complaint has merit, give serious consideration to a settlement. Avoid the reflexive position that will saddle you with the consequences of an unauthorized and illegal act of an employee. Simply stated, do not allow a personal grudge or the discriminatory bias of one employee to become a company problem.

THE FACT-FINDING CONFERENCE

If the agency decides to proceed with the investigation, the next step is a fact-finding conference before an agency investigator. Most investigators are working under heavy caseloads, so there is often a hiatus of several months between the receipt of the employer's response to the questionnaire and the scheduling of the investigatory conference. This delay can work to your advantage, so make the most of it.

The conference is the first opportunity for the employee and the employer to confront each other in the presence of an investigator. You must prepare carefully for the conference as it will be your last real opportunity to avoid a finding of probable cause and the ensuing administrative hearing. Most investigators are receptive to a well-prepared defense. They are not as interested in proving a complaint as in arriving at a supportable decision. The employer's attorney may attend the conference but is not allowed to cross-examine the complainant or witnesses. Counsel's role is to direct the scope of the questions asked by the investigator and to present the employer's defense.

HANDLING REQUESTS FOR INFORMATION

A flat refusal to produce requested information will almost guarantee a finding of probable cause, but producing too much information can also cause trouble.

Figure 5.1 Investigatory Questionnaire

STATE DIVISION OF HUMAN RIGHTS· DOCUMENT AND
· INFORMATION REQUESTED
On the complaint(s) of   · FOR INVESTIGATION OR
· DENIAL OF EQUAL TERMS,
JOHN DOE,   COMPLAINANT(S) · CONDITIONS, AND
· PRIVILEGES OF
vs.   · EMPLOYMENT COMPLAINT
· CASE NUMBER
ABC CO.,   RESPONDENT   ·
·
·
·

To:

Please take notice that you are to supply one original and one copy of the following to the New York State Division of Human Rights on or

before _____ 198_____

A. A written narrative reply to each numbered paragraph of the complaint.

B. *Document Request* (If the request has an "a" section and "b" section, answer "a" for denial of promotion complaints and "b" for difference in treatment complaints.)

_____ 1. Provide a copy of all documents contained in the entire personnel folder of the complainant or such other file maintained for personnel purposes as you may keep.

_____ 2a. Provide a copy of any job posting and a job description for the position which the complainant wanted promotion to. If there is no written description describe in detail the duties of and the requirements for the position.

_____ 2b. Provide a copy of respondent's policy and procedure manual which is applicable to the matter complained of (i.e., shop rules, disciplinary procedures, etc.). If none exists, describe in detail.

_____ 3a. Provide copies of all documents contained in the entire personnel folders of the people considered for the promotion or such files maintained for personnel purpose as you may keep.

Figure 5.1 *(Continued)*

_____ 3b. Provide copies of all documents contained in the entire personnel folders of employees who have been treated similarly to the complainant such other files maintained for personnel purposes as you may keep.

_____ 4. Submit the EEO-1 Report form for the following year(s):

_____ 5. Submit all forms used in: (a) requesting references for prospective employees and (b) preparing reference replies for past or current employees.

C. *Information Request* (If the request has an "a" section and a "b" section answer "a" for denial of promotion complaints and "b" for difference in treatment complaints.)

_____ 1a. State the specific reason(s) why the complainant was not promoted (attach additional sheets if necessary).

_____ 1b. State the specific reason(s) for the treatment received by the complainant.

_____ 2a. State the (i) name, (ii) address, (iii) telephone number, (iv) race, (v) age, (vi) job title, and (vii) length of service of each person who participated in the decision to not promote the complainant and to promote the successful candidate. Indicate the role that each person played in the decision.

_____ 2b. State the (i) name, (ii) address, (iii) telephone number, (iv) race, (v) age, (vi) job title and (vii) length of service of each person who participated in the treatment received by the complainant. Indicate the role that each person played.

_____ 3. Were any warnings made to the complainant? If so, state the date(s), person(s) present, and the circumstances under which such warnings were made. Attach copies of all records of such warnings and specify respondent's policy with respect to them.

_____ 4a. State the (i) name, (ii) address, (iii) telephone number, (iv) date of hire, and (v) race, creed, color, national origin, age, and sex of all employees holding the job which the complainant wanted promotion to.

Figure 5.1 *(Continued)*

_____ 4b. State the (i) name, (ii) address, (iii) telephone number, (iv) date of hire and race, creed, color, national origin, age and sex of all employees holding the same job as the complainant.

_____ 5a. How many employees have been given a same or similar promotion to the one that the complainant was interested in? State the (i) name, (ii) date of hire, (iii) original title, (iv) date of promotion and (v) new job title. Limit to the last 24 months.

_____ 5b. How many employees have been given warnings or penalties or the type of treatment which gave rise to this complaint? State the (i) name, (ii) date of hire, (iii) job title, (iv) penalty, and (v) circumstances. Limit to the last 24 months.

_____ 6. What performance standards was complainant expected to meet? What standards did complainant fail to meet?

_____ 7. Did the complainant ever complain about receiving discriminatory treatment on the job? If so, specify the nature of the complaint(s), date(s) of complaint(s), the person(s) involved, and explain what was done pursuant to the complaint(s).

_____ 8. Name the person with authority to make settlement decision(s) for the respondent:

_____

Name and Title of Person Completing Inquiry

I HEREBY CERTIFY THAT I HAVE AUTHORITY TO ANSWER THE INQUIRY ON BEHALF OF RESPONDENT.

_____

Signature

_____

(Area Code)   Telephone Number

_____

Date Completed

Source: Reprinted with permission from *The Employee Termination Handbook*, edited by J. G. Allen. New York: John Wiley & Sons, 1986, pp. 192–193.

It goes without saying that an employer does not have to reveal information that is not in his or her possession. With this in mind, reevaluate the records you are preserving. Don't discard all personnel information, but take inventory of what types of employee records you are keeping and whether they are truly beneficial to the company. If any of the records are neither necessary for business purposes nor required by state or federal regulations, consider discarding them.

Personnel departments want to maintain a complete file on each employee, but be wary lest those files be used against you. Consider whether you want to retain evaluations that are more than three years old. There is nothing more defeating to an employer's defense of a claim than ten years' worth of "excellent" performance appraisals.

Because performance appraisals may one day be the object of an EEO agency's investigation, instruct your supervisors and managers to complete them candidly. A mediocre employee should receive an "unsatisfactory" or "poor" rating on the performance report. The supervisor should include a comment to the effect that "Mr X is a poor performer, but I recommend he be retained in his present position to give him a chance to improve." If a poor performer receives a salary increase, a note should be made that "the raise is intended only to keep pace with inflation and should not be interpreted as a merit-based increase."

THE CONCILIATION PROCESS

When the investigation is complete, the investigating commissioner will decide whether there is probable cause to believe that the employer has discriminated unlawfully against the employee. If there is no probable cause, the complaint will be dismissed.

If probable cause is found, the EEO agency will try to resolve the matter through a formal process called conciliation. The conciliation agreement states the terms of the settlement and affirms that the complainant had probable cause for taking action.

THE ADMINISTRATIVE HEARING

If conciliation fails, the matter will be decided at an administrative hearing before an administrative law judge of the state EEO agency. Although less formal than a court proceeding, the administrative hearing is similar to a trial in that witnesses are examined and cross-examined and documentary evidence, such as personnel files, is introduced.

Unlike a courtroom judge, an administrative judge has no enforcement powers of his or her own. However, the administrative judge has greater power to participate in the hearing than a judge has to participate in a court trial. The administrative law judge is not restricted to simply making decisions on procedural questions but may actively engage in examination of witnesses.

The administrative hearing is not held in a court but usually in one of the offices of the state EEO agency. Prior to the hearing, the administrative law judge knows nothing of the case except for the initial complaint and the answer. The hearing itself is conducted without any reference to the investigation. Although an attorney is not required, most employers bring one along.

Unlike a court trial, which often involves months or even years of preparation, the employer usually has only a few weeks to prepare for the administrative hearing. The employer receives notice of the hearing only two to four weeks before the scheduled hearing date. Requests for adjournment at this point, even if granted, cannot be expected to delay the hearing for more than a month or two. When you receive notice of an administrative hearing, preparation must begin immediately.

Your preparation for the hearing should consist of:

- Consulting the records of your previous in-house investigation.
- Preparing your witnesses.
- Preparing charts, graphs, and other documentary evidence (e.g., graphing salary increases or financial difficulties in the company) to illustrate your case.
- Responding to possible subpoenas from the EEO agency.

When the hearing is concluded, the administrative law judge will send a recommended decision to the parties or their attorneys, with notification that they may submit written objections to the decision within a specified time. The issuance of a recommended decision is generally the last involvement of the administrative law judge in the matter.

The findings of the administrative law judge are subject to the ultimate decision of the commissioner or the administrative chief of that agency. In about 90 percent of the cases, the commissioner's final order will affirm the administrative law judge's recommended decision. If the complaint is sustained, the agency will order legal relief to the employee, including back pay and reinstatement.

STATUTES OF LIMITATIONS

Statutes of limitations are critical in EEO actions because there is not just one, but two, and sometimes three different statutes of limitations as a result of the intricate interplay of state and federal laws. Each must be met for the plaintiff to continue the action.

The first statute of limitations for Title VII actions has already been mentioned—180 or 300 days, depending on the state.

The second statute of limitations governs when the EEOC will issue a right-to-sue letter. Generally, the EEOC has 180 days after the charge has been filed to investigate the complaint and issue a right-to-sue letter.

The third statute of limitations concerns the time within which the Title VII plaintiff must begin action in federal court upon receipt of the right-to-sue letter. The employee must begin his or her Title VII action in federal court within 90 days upon receipt of the right-to-sue letter. It is important to remember that even though the EEOC is a federal agency, filing a complaint with the EEOC is not the same as bringing the case to federal court. The complaint to the agency is not automatically transformed into a federal court complaint.

Also keep in mind that 42 out of 50 states have state EEO agencies and state fair employment laws. The statute of limitations on when a complaint may be filed varies according to the state and ranges from a minimum of 30 days to a maximum of one year. Table 5.1 lists the states and their respective statutes of limitations under applicable state fair employment laws.

RELATIONSHIP OF THE ADA TO OTHER LAWS

Employers' actions may also violate the Rehabilitation Act of 1973 (applicable to companies with federal contracts of $2,500 or more and recipients of federal aid) and state handicapped discrimination laws. Because individuals cannot sue federal contractors under the Rehabilitation Act, the only added danger of a Rehabilitation Act violation is an investigation by the Department of Labor's Office of Federal Contract Compliance Programs and possible loss of government contracts.

Table 5.1 State EEO Agencies and Statutes of Limitations Under State EEO Laws

State and State EEO Law	State EEO Law Y/N	Provides for Investigation and Public Hearing Procedure—Y/N	Statute of Limitations Under State EEO Laws
Alabama	N	. . .	. . .
Alaska			
Alaska State Laws Against Discrimination	Y	Y	300 days
Arizona			
Arizona Civil Rights Act	Y	Y	180 days
Arkansas	N	. . .	. . .
California			
California Fair Employment Practices and Housing Act	Y	Y	1 year
Colorado			
Colorado Antidiscrimination Act	Y	Y	6 months
Connecticut			
Connecticut Fair Employment Practices Act	Y	Y	180 days
Delaware			
Delaware Fair Employment Practices Act	Y	Y	90 days
Florida			
Florida Human Rights Act	Y	Y	180 days
Georgia			
No comprehensive statute	Y	Y	180 days
Hawaii			
Hawaii Fair Employment Practices Act	Y	Y	30 days

Table 5.1   *(Continued)*

State and State EEO Law	State EEO Law Y/N	Provides for Investigation and Public Hearing Procedure—Y/N	Statute of Limitations Under State EEO Laws
Idaho			
Idaho Fair Employment Practices Act	Y	N	1 year
Illinois			
Illinois Human Rights Act	Y	Y	180 days
Indiana			
Indiana Civil Rights Law	Y	Y	90 days
Iowa			
Iowa Civil Rights Law	Y	Y	180 days
Kansas			
Kansas Act Against Discrimination	Y	Y	6 months
Kentucky			
Kentucky Fair Employment Practices Act	Y	Y	180 days
Louisiana	N	. . .	. . .
Maine			
Maine Human Rights Act	Y	N	6 months
Maryland			
Maryland Fair Employment Practices Act	Y	Y	6 months
Massachusetts			
Massachusetts Fair Employment Practices Law	Y	Y	6 months
Michigan			
Michigan Civil Rights Act	Y	Y	180 days
Minnesota			
Minnesota Human Rights Act	Y	Y	300 days

Table 5.1   *(Continued)*

State and State EEO Law	State EEO Law Y/N	Provides for Investigation and Public Hearing Procedure—Y/N	Statute of Limitations Under State EEO Laws
Mississippi	N	. . .	. . .
Missouri			
Missouri Fair Employment Practices Act	Y	Y	180 days
Montana			
Montana Human Rights Act	Y	Y	180 days
Nebraska			
Nebraska Fair Employment Practices Act	Y	Y	180 days
Nevada			
Nevada Fair Employment Practices Act	Y	Y	180 days
New Hampshire			
New Hampshire Law Against Discrimination	Y	Y	180 days
New Jersey			
New Jersey Law Against Discrimination	Y	Y	180 days
New Mexico			
New Mexico Human Rights Act	Y	Y	1 year
New York			
New York Human Rights Law	Y	Y	1 year
North Carolina	N	. . .	. . .
North Dakota	N	. . .	. . .
Ohio			
Ohio Fair Employment Practices Law	Y	Y	6 months

Table 5.1   *(Continued)*

State and State EEO Law	State EEO Law Y/N	Provides for Investigation and Public Hearing Procedure—Y/N	Statute of Limitations Under State EEO Laws
Oklahoma			
Oklahoma Civil Rights Act	Y	Y	180 days
Oregon			
Oregon Fair Employment Practices Act	Y	Y	1 year
Pennsylvania			
Pennsylvania Human Relations Act	Y	Y	90 days
Rhode Island			
Rhode Island Fair Employment Practices Act	Y	Y	1 year
South Carolina			
South Carolina Human Affairs Law	Y	Y	180 days
South Dakota			
South Dakota Human Relations Act	Y	Y	180 days
Tennessee			
Tennessee Fair Employment Practices Law	Y	Y	180 days
Texas			
Texas Commission on Human Rights Act	Y	N	180 days
Utah			
Utah Antidiscriminatory Act	Y	Y	180 days
Vermont	N	. . .	. . .
Virginia	N	. . .	. . .

Table 5.1   *(Continued)*

State and State EEO Law	State EEO Law Y/N	Provides for Investigation and Public Hearing Procedure—Y/N	Statute of Limitations Under State EEO Laws
Washington			
Washington Law Against Discrimination	Y	Y	6 months
West Virginia			
West Virginia Human Rights Act	Y	Y	90 days
Wisconsin			
Wisconsin Fair Employment Act	Y	Y	300 days
Wyoming			
Wyoming Fair Employment Practices Act	Y	Y	90 days
District of Columbia			
District of Columbia Human Rights Law	Y	Y	1 year

Source: Reprinted with permission from *The Employee Termination Handbook*, edited by J. G. Allen. New York: John Wiley & Sons, 1986, pp. 172–174.

State laws, on the other hand, can substantially increase the damages a private plaintiff collects in an ADA lawsuit. The ADA does not preempt any state laws or municipal ordinances that provide greater protection for individuals with disabilities than does the ADA. Many state handicapped laws allow for added damages, although the exact types of damages provided vary from state to state. For example, the New Jersey Law Against Discrimination allows compensation for pain and suffering, emotional distress, and punitive damages in addition to the federal remedies. Oregon law provides compensation for emotional distress or "impaired personal dignity," while Tennessee's law provides for damages for "humiliation and embarrassment." Lawsuits that combine actions based on the ADA and state handicapped laws are allowed only under certain circumstances.[1]

Because the EEOC is responsible for enforcing both the ADA and the Rehabilitation Act of 1973, the law stipulates that administrative complaints filed under either piece of legislation must be dealt with in a way that avoids duplication of efforts or conflicting standards. Agencies with enforcement authority are expected to develop procedures and coordination mechanisms.

A TIDE OF LITIGATION?

The EEOC expects some 15,000 new job-bias complaints against employers during the first year in which the disability act takes effect, but it also expects many complaints to be summarily rejected.

Because of budget constraints, the commission may not be able to hire the 250 new compliance officers it expects to need to investigate complaints under the ADA, so enforcement is likely to be slow.

Even some advocates for the disabled want to avoid litigation. Paul Marchand, chairman of the Consortium for Citizens with Disabilities, a Washington-based lobbying group, is quoted in *The New York Times* as saying: "We are not out to clobber anybody. We hope it [litigation] would be the last resort. It makes no sense to put businesses out of business."[2]

TYPICAL CHARGES AND DEFENSES

The recap below is adapted from a manual published by the Bureau of National Affairs.[3]

CHARGE: A less-qualified person was hired over a more-qualified disabled person.

DEFENSE: After considering all reasonable accommodations, you must prove that the disabled person is less qualified.

---

[1] James G. Frierson, *Employer's Guide to the Americans with Disabilities Act* (Washington, DC: The Bureau of National Affairs, 1992), 209–210.

[2] Peter Kilborn, "Change Likely as Law on Bias to Disabled Takes Effect." *New York Times*, 19 July 1992, sec. I.

[3] Frierson, *Employer's Guide to the Americans with Disabilities Act*, 201–206.

CHARGE: An employer-provided health or life insurance policy discriminates against a disabled employee.

DEFENSE: You must prove that the limitation or denial of coverage is based upon normal insurance industry standards of risk, including exclusion for preexisting conditions. It is not necessary to show that all medical conditions are covered equally as long as the benefits are the same for all employees in the complainant's job category. (See Chapter 2.)

CHARGE: A job applicant or employee was discriminated against because of past drug use.

DEFENSE: You have two possible lines of defense here: (1) to show that the individual is still using drugs, or (2) to show that your treatment was based upon valid job criteria such as work quality, productivity standards, or attendance requirements.

CHARGE: Your company uses job qualifications or employment tests to screen out qualified disabled people.

DEFENSE: You must prove that your standards and tests measure essential job skills that are consistent with business necessity, and that reasonable accommodations were provided to allow the applicant to show his or her qualifications.

CHARGE: A disabled applicant was unable to interview effectively for a job or take a qualifying examination either because of physical barriers or because of his inability to take the test in a particular format.

DEFENSE: Your defenses in this realm are limited because all employment tests and selection criteria must be administered in a way that does not automatically screen out disabled people. You can either show that the person never attempted to qualify for the job or that the applicant did not ask for any accommodations.

CHARGE: An employer asked about health, disability, or past medical problems before making a job offer.

DEFENSE: You must prove that your questions related only to the applicant's ability to perform *essential job functions*. You are, however, permitted to test for illegal drug use before making a job offer because current drug users are not a protected class under the ADA's definition of disability. (See Chapter 1.)

CHARGE: An employer required a physical examination after making a tentative offer of employment, and the information was used in a way that was detrimental to a disabled applicant.

DEFENSE: You must prove that: (1) the examination was required of all employees, (2) any resulting decision was based upon legitimate proof that the person could not effectively and safely perform the essential tasks of the job, and (3) the information was kept confidential.

CHARGE: A person who has acquired immunodeficiency syndrome (AIDS) or who tests positive for the human immunodeficiency virus (HIV) claims he or she was discriminated against in hiring or other employment benefits.

DEFENSE: You must either prove that your actions were not based upon the medical condition or that the condition created a health or safety risk to coworkers or customers. The latter is very difficult to prove, even in the case of food service workers or elementary-school teachers. It might be a viable defense in some health care jobs. (See Chapter 2.)

CHARGE: An individual was not hired or was not promoted because of an inability to perform certain job tasks.

DEFENSE: You must prove that the tasks in question are essential duties of the job and that eliminating them would change the fundamental nature of the job, lower productivity, or produce a poorer result. (See Chapter 4.)

CHARGE: The employer failed to provide a reasonable accommodation for a disabled employee.

DEFENSE: You must show that the accommodation would create an undue hardship on the business, would present a threat to health or safety, or would not enable the person to perform the essential duties of the job. (See Chapter 6.)

CHARGE: Disabled workers are segregated or otherwise restricted or classified in a way that limits their opportunity or status in the company.

DEFENSE: Usually none. Different rates of pay, separate seniority lists, or separate physical facilities based upon disability are illegal. However, an employer may limit a disabled person to one section of the facility if the structural changes needed to improve access to other sections would present an undue hardship. (See Chapter 6.)

CHARGE: The employer did not provide information on the ADA.

DEFENSE: Show that the current Consolidated EEO Poster, which includes information on the ADA, was posted in a place where job applicants and employees would be expected to see it. If available, use a poster printed in large print and braille to prove that it was accessible to those with vision problems.

CHARGE: A business's goods and services are not physically accessible to customers or clients.

DEFENSE: If the building was constructed before January 26, 1993, or renovated before January 26, 1992, you must show that the necessary changes were not readily achievable. If the building was constructed for first occupancy after January 6, 1993, or major modifications were begun after January 26, 1992, the structure must comply with the regulations promulgated by the U.S. attorney general. (See Chapters 7 and 8.)

CHARGE: Work areas, cafeterias, restrooms, water fountains, and other common areas in the workplace are not physically accessible to workers with disabilities.

DEFENSE: If the building was not completed after January 26, 1993, or substantially renovated since January 26, 1992, you must prove that the cost of making changes is an *undue burden* on the employer. (See Chapter 7.) If the structure was built or renovated after these dates, the only defense would be compliance with the U.S. attorney general's accessibility regulations.

PART TWO

Employing the Disabled

CHAPTER SIX

Reasonable Accommodations under Title I

The reasonable accommodations requirement is at the heart of the Americans with Disabilities Act (ADA). Most questions—and most misconceptions—about the law center around this concept. Small businesses, in particular, are concerned about its economic implications in terms of capital expenses and loss of productivity. They are worried about having to hire additional staff to assist disabled employees and having to make structural changes to the workspace to allow for access.

The reasonable accommodations requirement is not meant to threaten a small business owner's livelihood. It is meant to remove employment barriers for people with disabilities. These barriers may be structural obstacles that inhibit the access to job sites or equipment; they may be rigid work schedules that dictate when work is performed; or they may be inflexible job procedures that limit the modes of communication that are used on the job or the way in which particular tasks are accomplished.

Under the ADA, an employer cannot select a qualified individual without a disability over an equally qualified individual with a disability merely because the individual with a disability will require a reasonable accommodation. In other words, an individual's need for an accommodation cannot enter into your decisions regarding hiring, discharge, or promotion unless the accommodation would impose an undue hardship on your business.

WHAT IS AN ACCOMMODATION?

An accommodation is any change in the work environment or in the way things are usually done that creates equal employment opportunity for an individual with a disability. There is nothing new or mysterious about accommodations. They are made daily at workplaces to assist workers without disabilities as well as those with disabilities. In fact, accommodations have been part of affirmative action and nondiscrimination requirements covering employment of people with disabilities since passage of the Rehabilitation Act of 1973.

Under Title I of the ADA, employers are obligated to provide reasonable accommodations to employees and job applicants in three areas:

- Accommodations that provide equal opportunity in the job application process.
- Accommodations that enable employees with disabilities to perform the essential functions of a position.
- Accommodations that allow employees with disabilities to enjoy the full benefits and privileges of employment.

The act defines reasonable accommodation as follows:

- Making existing facilities used by employees readily accessible to and usable by individuals with disabilities.
- Restructuring jobs; establishing part-time or modified work schedules; reassigning a disabled worker to a vacant position; acquiring or modifying equipment or devices; making appropriate adjustments or modifications of examinations, training materials, or policies; providing qualified readers or interpreters; and making other similar accommodations.

As you can see, accommodations cut a wide swath. Like the barriers mentioned earlier, some are structural in nature while others are administrative. In this chapter we shall examine administrative accommodations. Structural accommodations will be covered in the following chapters.

The obligation to make reasonable accommodation applies to all services and programs provided in connection with employment, and to all nonwork facilities that an employer provides for its employees. This includes employer-sponsored placement or counseling services and employer-provided cafeterias, lounges, gymnasiums, auditoriums, and transportation.

Job Restructuring

The key to job restructuring is flexibility. While essential functions need not be eliminated, nonessential elements can be assigned to another employee, as discussed in Chapter 4. If essential duties cannot be performed or reassigned, a disabled individual need not be hired.

Example _____

Suppose a security guard position requires the individual to inspect identification cards. An employer would not have to provide an individual who is legally blind with an assistant to look at the cards because, in this situation, the assistant would be *performing* the job rather than *assisting* the individual.

A job can also be restructured by altering when and how an essential function is performed. For example, an essential function customarily performed in the early morning may be rescheduled until later in the day. An employee with an impairment that limits the ability to write may be permitted to computerize records that were previously maintained manually. Typical job restructuring accommodations include:

• **Job rotation.** A worker with limited strength or endurance for a specific job task can rotate to an alternate job that does not require the same physical exertion.

• **Sequencing.** An assembly worker with a learning disability can assemble the product when the pieces are presented in a set sequence: for example, parts can be organized in numbered boxes.

• **Job expansion.** A video display terminal (VDT) operator with a cumulative trauma disorder can do the support work (filing, copying, phone) for one manager rather than the VDT data entry for four managers.

Modified Work Schedules

Some people with disabilities require modified work schedules because they need regular medical treatment or because they must depend on transportation that limits their hours of travel. While the ADA does not demand that employers abandon all attendance and punctuality rules, those rules must be applied carefully and with an understanding of the law. You are not expected to provide additional paid sick leave to disabled employees, but you may have to provide additional unpaid leave as a reasonable accommodation.

Example _____

A worker recovering from cancer needs one day off a week to receive chemotherapy. A four-day workweek, 10 hours per day, would accommodate this.

Reassignment to a Vacant Position

In general, reassignment should be considered only when accommodation within the individual's current position would pose an undue hardship on the business. Reassignment is not available to job applicants. Applicants must be able to perform the essential functions of the position they are seeking, with or without reasonable accommodation. An employer may not limit, segregate, or otherwise discriminate against employees with disabilities by forcing reassignment to undesirable positions or to designated offices.

The individual should be reassigned to an equivalent position in terms of pay and status if he or she is qualified and if the position is vacant within a reasonable amount of time. An individual can be reassigned to a lower graded position if there are no accommodations that would enable the employee to remain in the current position and there are no vacant equivalent positions for which he or she is qualified. An employer is *not* required to maintain the reassigned individual at the salary of the higher graded position or to promote someone with a disability to a higher graded position for which he or she is not qualified.

In either case, remember that it is only necessary to reassign an employee to a *vacant* position. *Another employee need not be bumped out of a position.*

Modification of Examinations, Training Materials, or Policies

As discussed in Chapter 4, a companywide policy that discriminates against individuals with disabilities must be modified under the ADA. A policy requiring all employees to hold a driver's license must be modified when applied to a person with a disability who can perform the essential functions of the job but cannot drive. Of course, if driving is an essential function of the job, a license may be required.

With regard to tests, a preemployment qualification test may have to be administered orally instead of in writing or more time may have to be allowed to accommodate a particular disability. Other alternatives include the administration of tests printed in large type or braille or by means of a reader or sign interpreter. Where it is not possible to test in an alternative format, the employer may be required, as a reasonable accommodation, to evaluate the skill to be tested in another manner (e.g., through an interview or through work experience requirements). This does not mean that an employer has to offer every applicant a choice of test format. It only requires that an employer provide, upon advance request, alternative, accessible tests to individuals with disabilities that impair the sensory, manual, or speaking skills needed to take the test—unless the tests are intended to measure those functions. The obligation to make reasonable accommodation extends to ensuring that the test site itself is accessible.

Modification of Equipment

Under the ADA, an employer must provide special or modified equipment as a reasonable accommodation to disabled employees or applicants. This includes:

- Electronic visual aids
- Braille materials
- Talking calculators
- Magnifiers
- Audio recordings
- Telephone handset amplifiers
- Telecommunications devices for the deaf

- Mechanical page turners
- Raised or lowered furniture

This obligation extends only to modifications that help the individual perform a particular job. It does *not* extend to items that are primarily for personal use outside of the job, such as prosthetic limbs, hearing aids, eyeglasses, wheelchairs, or guide dogs. Keep in mind, though, that you may have to provide such items if they are specifically designed to meet job-related needs.

Example _____

You may have to provide an individual who has a visual impairment with glasses specially designed to enable the person to use the office computer monitors but that are not otherwise needed outside of the office. Or you may have to fit an individual with a special prosthetic arm that allows him or her to grasp and move items as an essential part of the job.

Readers or Interpreters

While it may be necessary to hire a reader or interpreter to assist an employee, the employer need not hire two people to do one job. If an interpreter or reader is required on only a part-time basis and the person can perform other work for the employer, his or her services may be reasonable. Because readers and interpreters are among the most expensive of the accommodations required by the ADA, the key to assessing whether they must be provided is the concept of undue hardship, which is discussed later in this chapter.

Other Accommodations

In addition to the specific reasonable accommodations listed in the ADA itself, the interpretive guidelines of the Equal Employment Opportunity Commission (EEOC) suggest the following:

- Permitting the use of accrued paid leave or providing additional unpaid leave for necessary treatment.
- Providing reserved parking spaces.
- Making employer-provided transportation accessible.

- Providing personal assistants such as page turners or travel attendants.
- Providing temporary job coaches to assist in training.

DEALING WITH UNIONS

The new law doesn't specify just how a unionized employer balances its ADA obligations against commitments imposed by a union contract or collective bargaining agreement. The ADA differs from Title VII because it does not exempt bona fide seniority systems from challenge under the act. This means that an employer is *not* free from legal obligations under the ADA merely because it has followed a seniority system under a labor contract. For example, it is not clear whether an employer may reassign an employee with a disability to a vacant position if a labor contract reserves certain jobs for employees with a given amount of seniority. If an employer decides to award a vacant job to an employee with a disability, it may be financially liable to a more senior worker for violating his or her rights under the labor contract.

With so many gray areas in the law, it makes sense to review all union contracts currently in force to determine if they contain any provisions that conflict with the ADA. An employer faced with obstacles to ADA compliance presented by a union or by a collective bargaining agreement must document the obstacles clearly if they are to form the basis of an adverse employment decision.

If your company will be negotiating a contract in the near future, consider proposing a broad management rights clause that allows the company to take whatever steps are necessary to comply with the ADA. Keep in mind, though, that the union may be reluctant to grant you such unspecified powers. In a report to locals of the International Union of Electrical, Radio and Machine Workers, the union president noted that:

> We strongly advise locals to be on their guard against proposals that grant the employer free rein to take "all actions necessary to comply with the act." Although such clauses may sound innocent enough, they could potentially be applied to exclude the union from the accommodation process and permit the employer to ignore hard-won seniority protections.[1]

---

[1] *President William Bywater's Report to the Executive Board of the IUE.* Washington, DC: International Union of Electrical, Radio and Machine Workers, 1992.

THE ACCOMMODATION PROCESS

Who Initiates the Process?

Generally, the employee is responsible for requesting an accommodation. An exception is an employee with a known disability who is having difficulty performing his or her job. In this case, you may ask if the person needs an accommodation.

Although the ADA does not allow you to question a job applicant about his or her disability, the applicant can choose to volunteer that information in order to obtain an accommodation. The sample Request for Accommodation form in Figure 6.1 can be used for both job applicants and current employees. Note that it gives examples of specific disabilities but allows the individual to explain the nature of his or her particular disability.

Handling Requests for Accommodation

No matter how small or informal your company might be, establish a clear-cut written procedure for requesting accommodations and distribute it to all employees. Post copies in lunchrooms, copier rooms, or coffee stations, and keep a copy in your files for reference. The general idea behind these procedures is to create a paper trail that will document your efforts in the event that a complaint is filed against you.

• Requests should be made in writing and submitted either directly to you or to your office/personnel manager. You might want to ask for medical records to document the nature or extent of the disability.

• Upon receipt of the request, evaluate the feasibility of the proposed accommodation and explore alternatives. Be sure to investigate whether financial or technical assistance is available to your company.

• Inform the person in writing of your decision. If you find that the requested accommodation is not viable, explain in detail the hardships it would pose, such as fundamentally altering the nature of the job, or creating a financial burden on the company. You might want your lawyer to review your response before sending it along to the employee.

• Keep copies of all requests and responses on file.

Figure 6.1 Voluntary Disclosure of Disability and Request for Accommodations

XYZ Company policy and the law prohibit the company from asking job applicants about disabilities or giving a health questionnaire or examination until after an initial job offer is made. Whether you are a job applicant or a current employee, you may want to *voluntarily* disclose physical or mental health conditions and ask for reasonable accommodations so that the company may consider possible changes that allow you to work at your full potential.

If you choose to do so, please complete and sign this form and return it to _____ . Information given on this form, or the failure to complete this form, will not be used to discriminate against you. The information will remain strictly confidential. Disclosure will be made only to those people who are needed to determine and implement reasonable accommodations.

The company is strongly committed to taking all reasonable steps to ensure that qualified applicants are hired and qualified employees are allowed to work to their full potential, despite physical or mental problems.

For the purposes of this form, a potential disability appropriate for disclosure is any physical or mental condition that creates, or might create, any difficulty in performing your job. This includes obvious disabilities such as paralysis or blindness; less obvious impairments such as epilepsy, diabetes, or heart problems; mental problems such as depression and eating disorders; learning problems such as dyslexia. Also included as impairments are acquired immunodeficiency syndrome (AIDS), human immunodeficiency virus (HIV), and other contagious diseases; persistent back problems; past drug addiction; past or current alcoholism; and other medical conditions.

* * *

Name _____

Position Applied for or Currently Held _____

Type of Disability (e.g., diabetes, amputation, cancer, high blood pressure)

_____

_____

Description of Physical or Mental Impairment (e.g., unable to walk, cannot do heavy lifting, sensitive to heat) _____

_____

_____

Figure 6.1 *(Continued)*

Suggested Accommodations (e.g., ramp over stairs, telephone amplifier, flexible work schedule) _____

_____

The company will consider your suggestions and attempt to make reasonable accommodations. However, the final decision regarding what accommodations are reasonable and desirable remain the sole discretion of the company. Please sign below.

Signed _____ Date _____

Source: From pp. 194–195 of the *Employer's Guide to the Americans with Disabilities Act* by James G. Frierson. Copyright © 1992, by The Bureau of National Affairs, Inc., Washington, DC 20037. Reprinted with permission.

There are two issues to address before deciding what accommodations you need to make for current or prospective employees. First, ask yourself whether the applicant is qualified for the position. Remember, the duty to make a reasonable accommodation applies only to individuals who are "otherwise qualified" to perform the job. Second, the act requires that reasonable accommodations be made only to *known* disabilities. Because the act restricts inquiries into disabilities, the duty to accommodate is usually triggered by a request from an employee or applicant.

It is unclear what an employer should do if a disabled individual is having problems on the job but does not request an accommodation. In this case, there is no indication in the ADA or congressional reports that the employer must provide an accommodation. However, given the possibility that a performance-related discharge could result in litigation, it is wise to document all discussions of accommodations before taking any adverse action against the employee.[2]

Choosing an Accommodation—A Problem-Solving Approach

The EEOC's regulations describe the reasonable accommodation process as a "problem-solving approach" that directly involves the em-

---

[2]Zachary Fasman, *What Business Must Know About the ADA: 1992 Compliance Guide* (Washington, DC: U.S. Chamber of Commerce, 1992), 22.

ployee in attempting to fashion an appropriate solution. The act provides that "damages may not be awarded ... where the covered entity demonstrates good faith efforts, *in consultation with the person with the disability* to identify and make a reasonable accommodation" [emphasis added].

A person usually knows exactly what he or she needs to perform a job, and this accommodation might be simpler and less expensive than one devised by the employer acting alone. So it makes sense to work with the employee to identify particular tasks that limit performance, focusing on both the needs of the individual and the nature of the job.[3]

Determining a Reasonable Accommodation

A four-step process can be used to determine if an accommodation is reasonable.

1. *Identify barriers to performance.* Ask the individual to pinpoint how the impairment limits his or her ability to fulfill specific job-related tasks. Take into account both essential and nonessential elements of the job, and consider reassigning or eliminating marginal duties.

2. *Consult with the employee to identify all possible accommodations; get outside help if necessary.* The search should begin with the employee. A number of other sources can help in this undertaking: state vocational rehabilitation agencies, practitioners in occupational medicine, other employers in the same industry, unions, or the employee's doctor. Conclusions reached by the doctor are not binding.

3. *Assess the reasonableness of each accommodation.* A reasonable accommodation should eliminate or minimize the limitation. It should give the person a chance to reach the same level of performance as a person without a disability.

4. *Choose an appropriate accommodation.* Taking into consideration the preferences of the individual, select and implement the accommodation that is best for both the employee *and* the company. If two suggested accommodations would work equally well, the employer can choose the one that is less expensive or easier to implement.

---

[3]Fasman, *What Business Must Know About the ADA.*

Reasonable Accommodation Process Illustrated. The following example illustrates the four-step process outlined above.

Suppose a sack handler position requires that the employee pick up 50-pound sacks and carry them from the loading dock to the storage room, and that a sack handler who is disabled by a back impairment requests a reasonable accommodation. Upon receiving the request, the employer analyzes the position and determines that its essential function and purpose is not to physically lift and carry the sacks but to transport them from the loading dock to the storage room.

The employer then meets with the sack handler to find out just how his disability limits his performance of the job's essential function of transporting the sacks. At this meeting the employer learns that the individual can lift the sacks to waist level but cannot carry them from the loading dock to the storage room. The employer and the individual agree that any of a number of accommodations, such as a dolly, hand truck, or cart, could enable the sack handler to transport the sacks.

Upon further consideration, it is determined that a cart is not a feasible option. No carts are currently available at the company, and those that can be purchased are the wrong shape to hold many of the bulky and irregularly shaped sacks that must be moved. Both the dolly and the hand truck, on the other hand, appear to be effective options, and both are readily available.

The employee indicates his preference for the dolly. In consideration of this preference, and because the employer feels that the man would be able to move more sacks at a time on a dolly than on a hand truck, the employer provides the sack handler with a dolly in fulfillment of the obligation to make reasonable accommodation.

Reasonable Versus Best

In many instances, the appropriate accommodation may be so obvious that it is not necessary to proceed in this step-by-step fashion. For example, if an employee who uses a wheelchair requests that his desk be placed on blocks to make room for the wheelchair and the employer complies, an appropriate accommodation has been requested, identified, and provided almost instinctively.

However, in some cases, the individual may not know enough about the nature of the work site or the equipment used on the job to suggest an appropriate accommodation. Likewise, the employer may not know enough about the individual's disability or the limitations it presents.

Under these circumstances, it may be necessary to engage in a more defined problem-solving approach to find an acceptable solution.

EEOC regulations state that: "The employer providing the accommodation has the ultimate discretion to choose between effective accommodations and may choose the less expensive accommodation or the accommodation that is easier for it to provide." An accommodation must be adequate to enable the individual to perform the essential functions of the job. It does not have to be the "best" accommodation possible as long as it is sufficient to meet the job-related needs of the individual. This means that you would not have to provide an employee who has a back impairment with a state-of-the-art mechanical lifting device if you provided a less-expensive or more readily available device that enabled the employee to perform the essential functions of the job.

Nonetheless, problems can arise when an employee or applicant is "forced" into an accommodation that he or she believes is unreasonable. Be sure to document your reasons for choosing an accommodation and be prepared to demonstrate the concrete problems—in cost or effectiveness—that caused you to reject the accommodation preferred by the employee.

If clear evidence of these problems is not available when the decision is made, it may be wise to offer the employee's preferred accommodation conditionally, reserving the right to insist upon another method if it disrupts the workplace or causes harm to the employee or others.

What Constitutes Failure to Make Reasonable Accommodation?

To establish that an employer unlawfully failed to provide a reasonable accommodation, it must be shown that:

1. A person with a disability was otherwise qualified for the position.
2. A reasonable accommodation existed that would have enabled the person to perform the essential functions of the job.
3. The accommodation was requested but not provided.

EMPLOYER DEFENSES

Health and Safety Risks

You need not hire someone who cannot perform the essential duties of the job without posing a direct threat to his or her own health or safety or that of others. The EEOC will consider the following factors in determining whether the individual poses a direct threat:

- The duration of the risk.
- The severity of the risk.
- The likelihood that the harm will occur.
- The imminence of the harm.

Employment decisions must be based on sound medical judgments, not on generalizations, irrational fears, or speculations. For example, fears about emergency evacuations or natural disasters cannot be invoked unless emergency response is an essential part of the job. The most important thing to remember is that every situation should be evaluated on a case-by-case basis.

Undue Hardship

Most disputes are likely to focus on whether or not the accommodation poses an undue hardship. The burden of proof in this matter rests with the employer, but the concept is not precisely defined in the ADA. The law states only that an undue hardship is "an action requiring significant difficulty or expense." Congressional reports emphasize that employers need not undertake actions that would be unduly costly, extensive, or disruptive.

EEOC regulations stipulate the factors that should be considered in determining an undue hardship:

- The nature and cost of the accommodation, taking into consideration the availability of outside funding and tax credits or deductions.

- The financial resources of the company or facility. If a large company operates several small facilities across the country, the ADA states that the courts should look at local resources as well as the financial resources of the entire enterprise, but it offers no formula for deciding what is more important.

- The impact of the accommodation upon the operation of the company.

- The nature of the business, including the size, composition, and structure of the work force. For example, a nightclub would not be required to accommodate an individual who can perform only in bright lighting if a change in the lighting would destroy the club's ambience or make it difficult to see the show.

• Aggregate accommodation costs. For example, an employer might earmark a certain portion of its earnings for accommodations and spend that amount on a first-come, first-served basis. Several expensive accommodations occurring early in the year might render the employer unable to respond to later requests even though they may be less costly than those already undertaken. This balance is a vital issue for employers, but it is not addressed by the ADA, the legislative debates, or the EEOC regulations.

EEOC guidelines also state that undue hardship may exist where "a particular accommodation would be unduly disruptive" to other employees or to the functioning of the business.

It is not easy for an employer to prove undue hardship.

• An employer must show that the cost is undue in comparison with the company's overall budget.

• Comparing the cost of the accommodation with the salary of the individual will not be sufficient to demonstrate undue hardship.

• An employer must take into account funding from tax deductions or credits arising from the accommodation as well as outside funding. If public funding is available, the employer's obligation extends to investigating and obtaining that funding. Cost thus refers only to the *net* cost of the accommodation.

• Even if an accommodation is too costly, an employer still must offer the accommodation and pay for its share if the employee or applicant is willing to pay for the part that exceeds the undue hardship standard.

Guidelines for Proving Undue Hardship

There are several steps that can be taken to support a claim of undue hardship:

1. *Demonstrate a willingness to try.* Consider trying an accommodation on an experimental basis. Then, if you find that it poses an undue hardship, you have actual experience to back you up.

2. *Document the process.* Document each step of the process of providing a reasonable accommodation. If the employee rejects an alternative accommodation, document this fact and the stated reasons.

3. *Maintain records of all accommodations.* A written record of all accommodations that you provided or attempted to provide will demonstrate that you take your obligations seriously and will help support a claim of undue hardship.

4. *Be consistent.* Consistency is vital because past actions may well establish a standard for future cases.

5. *Document attempts to obtain public funding.* Ensure that all sources of public funding have been investigated and exhausted.

6. *Document all aspects of your organization's size, budget, or operations resulting in undue hardship.* You must do more than show that the accommodation will make things more difficult. Without clear proof of specific problems that will be caused by the accommodation— the impact on other employees or the public, the consequences of a significant loss of efficiency, or the cost in relation to your company's overall budget—an undue hardship claim will be difficult to support.[4]

THE COST OF ACCOMMODATION

According to a 1987 Harris Poll, 74 percent of top management regard accommodations as either "not too expensive" or "not expensive at all."

Case in point: Friendly's restaurant in Muncy, Pennsylvania, has employed dozens of people with disabilities over the past several years and has found that most job accommodations were quite simple. One dishwasher using a wheelchair needed a plastic apron to keep dry while sorting silverware. The manager communicated with two deaf employees on a notepad rather than by speaking. In 1986, the manager of the restaurant, Nancy Merrick, received a White House award for her efforts in employing the disabled. "Each person is a different challenge," she says.[5]

---

[4]Fasman, *What Business Must Know About the ADA*, 29–30.
[5]Bradford McKee, "Disability Rules Target Job Bias." *Nation's Business*, June 1992.

The challenge of reasonable accommodation is largely one of creativity. The Friendly's restaurant experience shows that the best solution is not necessarily the most costly. In fact, the data base listings of the Job Accommodation Network (JAN) indicate that many accommodations cost less than $100, with an average cost of only $32 (see Figure 6.2). According to JAN:

- 31 percent of accommodations suggested cost nothing.
- 19 percent cost less than $50.
- 19 percent cost from $50 to $500.
- 19 percent cost from $500 to $1,000.
- 11 percent cost from $1,000 to $5,000.
- 1 percent cost more than $5,000.

Obviously, this includes many low-tech or no-tech items, and these are valid accommodations. But even high-tech solutions are not always expensive. For about $200, a computer can be equipped to read out loud virtually anything appearing on its screen; another device attached to a personal computer allows a deaf employee to make and receive phone calls.

JAN is an information and consulting resource developed by and for employers. Through JAN, it is relatively simple to determine the cost of individual items that serve as accommodations to the limitations of workers. For specific information, call 1-800/JAN-7234.

MANAGING DISABILITIES

In mapping out a strategy for complying with the ADA, many employers focus on the hiring process: What kinds of medical examinations can I require? What kinds of questions can I ask in an interview? Will I have to change a job to accommodate a disabled applicant?

In reality, though, most disabling illnesses and accidents occur after a person is on the job. Thus, a well-thought-out disability management program ought to be a cornerstone of your ADA compliance strategy. Disability management focuses on rehabilitating, accommodating, and returning disabled employees to work. An effective program can lower a company's worker's compensation costs, disability payments, and job turnover rates.

For example, Federal Express's disability management program saved the company $4 million in the first year of operation. Similarly,

Figure 6.2   Typical Equipment-Related Job Accommodations

Modifications of Existing Equipment

- A plant worker who was hearing impaired was able to use a telephone amplifier designed to work in conjunction with hearing aids, allowing him to retain his job. Approximate cost: $25.
- A receptionist who was blind was provided with a light probe that enabled her to determine which lines on the telephone were ringing, on hold, or in use. Approximate cost: $45.
- A computer operator with an eye disorder was provided with an antiglare screen. Approximate cost: $40.
- A groundskeeper who had recovered from a stroke had limited use of one arm and was unable to rake the grass. A detachable extension arm on the rake allowed him to control the tool with his functional arm. Approximate cost: $20.

New Equipment—Standard

- A company rented a headset for a phone that allowed an insurance salesperson with cerebral palsy to write while using the telephone.
- An individual with use of only one hand needed to use a camera as part of his job, but a tripod was too cumbersome. By using a waist pod (such as those used to carry flags), he was able to manipulate the camera and keep his job. Approximate cost: $50.
- A clerk with limited use of her hands was provided with a "lazy Susan" file folder so that she would not have to reach across her desk. Approximate cost: $85.
- A timer with an indicator light allowed a medical technician who was deaf to perform the lab tests required for her job. Approximate cost: $30.
- A one-handed individual working in a food service position was able to perform all required job tasks except opening cans. Purchase of a one-handed can opener enabled her to perform that remaining task. Approximate cost: $35.
- A light installed at the door of a company alerted the security guard that an employee who used a wheelchair was approaching and needed assistance with the door. Approximate cost: $50.
- A police officer with dyslexia had trouble filling out forms at the end of the day. Providing him with a tape recorder and designating a secretary to type out his reports allowed him to continue his job.

Figure 6.2   *(Continued)*

Custom Equipment

- An individual who was short statured was fitted with special seating so that he could drive a heavy loading machine for a construction company.
- An employee who had worked for 17 years was fitted with a portable air-purifying respirator to alleviate recently acquired allergic reactions to dust and aerosol sprays.
- A worker with a back injury was supplied with an adjustable-height table to allow for easier manipulation of materials.
- A housekeeper in a motel who had bending restrictions needed to inspect under the beds when she cleaned rooms. A mirror on an extending wand and a reacher allowed her to inspect and reach any items under the bed.
- A radio dispatcher with retinitis pigmentosa (a degenerative eye disease) needed to dial a great many telephone numbers in a hurry. A personal computer with an automatic dialing modem and a voice-synthesis system allowed the dispatcher to handle the calls.
- A logger had lost two fingers on his dominant hand. By using a glove with a built-in wrist support, he was able to continue using his chain saw.
- A special chair was provided for a district sales agent who had a back injury.

Zero-Cost Solutions

- Turnstiles to the cafeteria were removed to allow people in wheelchairs to enter the facility.
- A person who used a wheelchair could not use the furniture in her office because the desk height was too low for the wheelchair to fit into. Raising the desk with wood blocks allowed extra space for the wheelchair, thus saving the expense of purchasing a special desk.
- The desk layout was changed from the right side to the left for a visually impaired data entry operator.
- Transferring materials from a vertical filing cabinet into a nearby lateral file enabled a clerk to perform her job from a wheelchair.

Source: JAN data base. Morgantown, W.V.: Job Accommodation Network, 1992.

SIMPLE PROCEDURES FOR A RETURN-TO-WORK PROGRAM

1. The personnel director or other appropriate officer of the company should visit the disabled employee as soon as practical to demonstrate concern and encourage an early return to work.
2. Always try to return the worker to his or her old job, even if accommodation or flexible work time is required. This reduces the complications to the disabled employee and gives the company the advantage of having a trained employee.
3. Use community resources. State or local vocational rehabilitation agencies and support groups may aid in a successful return to work with little or no expense to the business.
4. Ask your worker's compensation, health, or disability insurance company for resources or payments for rehabilitative services or necessary accommodations.
5. Make a special effort to educate the disabled person's physician about the requirements of the job and possible changes and accommodations.

Source: From p. 222 of the *Employer's Guide to the Americans with Disabilities Act* by James G. Frierson. Copyright © 1992, by The Bureau of National Affairs, Inc., Washington, DC 20037. Reprinted with permission.

Sprague Electric Company of Concord, New Hampshire, reduced annual worker's compensation costs from $350,000 to $40,000 in just two years. It reduced the rate of days lost per injury from 6.5 days to 1 day.

True, these are large companies, but the ADA makes it important for even small businesses to consider implementing return-to-work and disability management programs as well. Smaller companies that cannot afford to have medical and rehabilitation experts on staff should consider the suggestions listed above.

TAX INCENTIVES

As mentioned earlier, there are numerous sources of public funding available to help small businesses comply with the ADA.[6]

---

[6]*Employees Are Asking About Making the Workplace Accessible to Workers with Disabilities.* Washington, DC: President's Committee on Employment of People with Disabilities, 1991.

The Disabled Access Credit

The Disabled Access Credit (DAC) took effect on November 5, 1990, and is now contained in Section 44 of the Internal Revenue Code. This new tax incentive is designed to encourage small businesses to comply with the Americans with Disabilities Act. The credit is equal to 50 percent of the "eligible access expenditures" of between $250 and $10,250, for a maximum credit of $5,000 a year. In the case of a partnership, the expenditure limitation will apply to the partnership and to each partner. Disabled access credits can be carried forward up to 15 years and back for 3 years, but not prior to the date of enactment.

An eligible small business is "any person" whose gross receipts did not exceed $1 million for the preceding taxable year, or who did not employ more than 30 full-time workers. "Full time" is defined as at least 30 hours per week for 20 or more calendar weeks in the taxable year.

"Eligible access expenditures" are "amounts paid or incurred by an eligible small business to comply with the applicable requirements" of the ADA. Included are expenditures for:

- Removing architectural, communications, physical, or transportation barriers that prevent a business from being accessible to, or usable by, individuals with disabilities.
- Providing qualified interpreters or other effective methods of making aurally delivered materials available to individuals with hearing impairments.
- Providing qualified readers, taped texts, and other effective methods of making visually delivered materials available to individuals with visual impairments.
- Acquiring or modifying equipment or devices for individuals with disabilities.
- Providing other similar services, modifications, materials, or equipment.

Expenses incurred for new construction are not eligible.

All expenditures must be "reasonable" and must meet the standards promulgated by the Internal Revenue Service with the concurrence of the Architectural and Transportation Barriers Compliance Board.

An eligible small business under Section 44 may deduct the difference between the disabled access credit claimed and the disabled access expenditures incurred, up to $15,000.

Architectural and Transportation Barrier Removal Deduction

This provision, contained in Section 190 of the Internal Revenue Code, allows businesses to deduct up to $15,000 for making a facility or public transportation vehicle that is owned or leased for use in the business more accessible to individuals with disabilities. In the case of a partnership, the $15,000 limit applies to the partnership and to each partner.

The deduction may not be used for expenses incurred for new construction, for a complete renovation of a facility or public transportation vehicle, or for the normal replacement of depreciable property.

For more information on DAC or Section 190 credits, contact a local IRS office or: Office of Chief Counsel, Internal Revenue Service, 1111 Constitution Avenue, NW, Washington, DC 20224, 202/566-3292.

Targeted Jobs Tax Credit

The Targeted Jobs Tax Credit (TJTC), contained in Section 51 of the Internal Revenue Code, was established in 1977. It offers employers a credit against their tax liability if they hire individuals from nine targeted groups, which include persons with disabilities. The credit is not available to employers of maids, chauffeurs, or other household employees.

The credit is equal to 40 percent of the first year's wages up to $6,000 per employee, for a maximum credit of $2,444 per employee for the first year of employment. Employers' deductions for wages must be reduced by the amount of the credit.

Individuals must be employed for at least 90 days or have completed at least 120 hours.

How to Apply for TJTC. To apply for the credit, the individual with a disability contacts the local state-federal vocational rehabilitation office to receive a voucher. The employer completes a portion of the voucher and mails it to the nearest local employment service office. That agency will send the employer a certificate that validates the tax credit. The employer uses this certificate when filing federal tax forms.

For more information on TJTC, contact the local state-federal vocational rehabilitation agency or the local employment service office.

Vocational Rehabilitation

The federal-state vocational rehabilitation program has a 71-year history of helping people with disabilities to enter the competitive work force.

Vocational rehabilitation agencies can be found in most cities. They are an excellent resource for employers seeking to recruit qualified employees with disabilities. They may also be helpful regarding job accommodations. They can conduct job analyses and provide rehabilitation engineering services for architectural barrier removal and work site modifications.

An on-the-job training program can be set up with an employer for an individual client of vocational rehabilitation. The agency can share in the payment of the employee's wages for a limited time on a negotiated schedule. The position must be permanent, full time, and pay above minimum wage.

For more information, contact your local vocational rehabilitation office.

Job Training Partnership Act

The Job Training Partnership Act (JTPA) replaces the Comprehensive Employment and Training Act (CETA). The program is administered by the governor's office in each state.

The act is a joint public-private sector venture to train and place individuals who are "economically disadvantaged" in the labor market. Disabled individuals can be considered economically disadvantaged if they meet the criteria set by the federal, state, or local welfare system.

JTPA can set up on-the-job training at a work site and reimburse an employer 50 percent of the first six months of wages for each eligible employee. Other JTPA services include: job recruiting, counseling in basic work skills, customized training programs, and services to those placed in unsubsidized jobs.

For more information, contact your local private industry council, chamber of commerce, or state government.

CHAPTER SEVEN

Title III and the Small Business Owner

In the previous chapter, we noted that the reasonable accommodation requirement for employers under Title I of the Americans with Disabilities Act (ADA) calls for workplace changes in two broad areas: (1) administrative and equipment-related modifications, and (2) structural modifications geared to "making existing facilities readily accessible to employees with disabilities."

The first requirement was explained in Chapter 6; the second point, concerning structural modifications, cuts across both Title I of the ADA, regulating employers, and Title III, regulating businesses. In this chapter and the next, we shall outline the general requirements of Title III as well as specific architectural specifications for making your facility accessible to the general public as well as employees.

OVERVIEW OF TITLE III

Title III of the ADA took effect on January 26, 1992. Its general intent is to enable individuals with disabilities to participate more fully in the mainstream of society through greater access to entertainment events, educational institutions, and commercial establishments ranging from restaurants to laundromats.

106

Title III imposes both affirmative and negative requirements on businesses:

- Nondiscrimination in providing goods and services.
- Modification of policies and procedures that discriminate against people with disabilities.
- Provision of auxiliary aids and services where needed.
- Removal of structural barriers if this is readily achievable.

Together, the law and its implementing regulations create a web of obligations designed to eliminate exclusion, segregation, and denial of opportunity on the basis of disabilities.

Let's examine these points one by one.

Nondiscrimination in Providing Goods and Services

Although the ADA grants persons with disabilities the right to participate in the goods and services offered in the marketplace, it does not require that such individuals achieve the same result as those in the general population. For example, although a person who uses a wheelchair could not be excluded from an exercise program for this reason, the instructor doesn't have to ensure that the individual can perform every exercise that the nondisabled participants can.

Outright exclusion is the most blatant form of discrimination in providing goods and services; however, discrimination also includes practices such as adopting criteria that impose an additional burden on people with disabilities. For instance, a theater or restaurant may not require people who use wheelchairs to be accompanied by an attendant.

The law also stipulates that the goods and services must be provided in the "most integrated setting appropriate to the needs of the individual." In practical terms, this means that seating in a restaurant cannot restrict people with disabilities to a certain section and that designated wheelchair positions cannot be located only in the back row of an auditorium. It is also discriminatory for a public accommodation to provide different or separate goods and services to people with disabilities. A gymnasium might offer special classes for children with limited mobility, but it cannot restrict children with such disabilities to those classes.

Modification of Policies and Procedures

This requirement is broader than the reasonable accommodation provision in Title I of the ADA and, in essence, requires that businesses remain flexible when applying their rules so as not to exclude the disabled. Modifications are required unless they would fundamentally alter the nature of the goods or services provided.

Examples

- A department store may need to modify its policy of permitting only one person in a dressing room if an individual with a disability needs assistance from a companion.

- A store with checkout aisles must ensure that enough accessible aisles are kept open. If only one checkout aisle is accessible and that aisle is generally used for express service, one way of providing equivalent service is to allow people with mobility impairments to make all of their purchases at the express aisle.

- A check-cashing requirement that a person have a driver's license for identification violates the ADA because it screens out people with disabilities who cannot drive.

- A restaurant or hotel that does not allow dogs must modify that rule for a service dog such as a Seeing Eye dog.

- A business need *not* expand its normal inventory to cater to individuals with disabilities. For example, stores are not expected to stock braille versions of books.

Auxiliary Aids and Services

Businesses must provide whatever devices or services are needed to ensure that individuals with disabilities can enjoy the goods and services of a business. One of the most common of these aids is a telecommunication device for the deaf (TDD). Other examples include:

- Readers
- Braille documents
- Interpreters
- Telephone handset amplifiers

- Telephones compatible with hearing aids
- Closed captions
- Decoders
- Taped texts
- Audio recordings
- Large-print materials

Which of these aids is necessary depends upon the nature of your business and the nature of the disability. As with Title I, a business is not required to provide its patrons with personal devices such as wheelchairs or hearing aids, nor is it required to provide personal service such as assistance in eating or using restrooms.

Removal of Architectural Barriers in Existing Facilities

This is another sweeping duty, although it is limited by what is "readily achievable," discussed later in this chapter. Justice Department regulations mention the following examples of barrier removals that may be required under Title III:

- Installing ramps and grab bars.
- Lowering telephones.
- Repositioning paper towel dispensers.
- Adding raised letters and braille markings on elevator controls.
- Adding flashing alarms.
- Widening doors.
- Making curb cuts in sidewalks and entrances.
- Eliminating turnstiles or providing an alternative path.
- Designating accessible parking spaces.
- Removing high-pile, low-density carpeting.
- Installing hand controls for driving vehicles.
- Insulating lavatory pipes under sinks to prevent burns.

Transportation barriers must also be removed in existing vehicles used for transporting individuals.

Examples

A business may be required to rearrange furniture and equipment, a restaurant may need to rearrange its tables, and a department store may have to adjust the layout of display racks and shelves. A bus company may have to install accessible luggage racks and a number of special seats for disabled passengers.

Recognizing that not all barriers can be removed immediately, Justice Department regulations suggest that they be removed in the following order:

1. Provide access to the premises from public sidewalks, parking areas, and public transportation by installing an entrance ramp, widening entrances, and providing accessible parking spaces.
2. Create physical and visual access to the areas where the goods and services are offered.
3. Improve access to restrooms by removing obstructing furniture or vending machines, widening doors, widening toilet stalls, and installing ramps and grab bars.
4. Take any other measures necessary to provide access to the goods and services.

Use of Alternative Methods

If the removal of a barrier is not readily achievable, a business must make its goods and services available through alternative methods. This might include, for example, providing help in retrieving items from densely packed display racks, coming to the door of a store to receive or return dry cleaning, or rotating movies between a first-floor accessible theater and a comparable second-floor inaccessible theater.

In some cases, perhaps for security reasons, an alternative method may not be readily achievable. The rule does not require cashiers to leave their posts to retrieve items for individuals with disabilities if no other employees are on duty. Again, flexibility and a willingness to make an extra effort will go a long way toward compliance.

WHO IS REGULATED UNDER TITLE III?

Title III affects a broad spectrum of businesses, from bowling alleys to day-care centers. It applies to public accommodations and commercial facilities as well as to public transportation provided by private entities. It does not cover government-operated facilities, private clubs, religious organizations, or owner-occupied inns with fewer than five rooms.

Large companies have had to comply with the law since January 26, 1992. For businesses with 25 or fewer employees and gross receipts of less than $1 million, the effective date was July 26, 1992. New buildings and businesses with 10 or fewer employees and gross revenues of less than $500,000 have until January 26, 1993.

WHAT IS A PLACE OF PUBLIC ACCOMMODATION?

Nearly all businesses that provide goods and services to the public fall within the ADA's definition of public accommodation. Congress did not enact a small business exemption to the public access provisions, so they apply fully to virtually all privately run businesses open to the public—regardless of size. There are 12 categories of public accommodations:

1. Hotels and other lodging places.
2. Restaurants, bars, and other places serving food or drink.
3. Movie theaters, concert halls, and stadiums.
4. Convention centers, lecture halls, and other meeting places.
5. Bakeries, grocery stores, clothing stores, hardware stores, videotape rental stores, and other sales or rental establishments.
6. Laundromats, dry cleaners, banks, barber and beauty shops, shoe repair shops, funeral parlors, gas stations, hospitals, offices of accountants and lawyers, medical offices, and other service establishments.
7. Terminals used for public transportation.
8. Museums, libraries, and galleries.
9. Parks, zoos, and other places of recreation.
10. Schools and other places of education.
11. Day-care centers, senior centers, homeless shelters, and other social service facilities.
12. Gymnasiums, Health Clubs, and Other Places of Exercise.

The Title III requirements apply only to those portions of a public accommodation that are open to the public. If you operate a dry-cleaning service and have your living quarters in the back, the part of the structure that is used as a residence is excluded from coverage. Or if you operate a retail store that is open to the public and a warehouse that is not, the public accommodation requirements apply only to the retail store. The warehouse would be considered a commercial facility.

WHAT IS A COMMERCIAL FACILITY?

Commercial facilities are an even broader group, encompassing all non-residential facilities affecting commerce. Factories, warehouses, and office buildings are within this definition.

Businesses with fewer than 15 employees are not regulated by Title I's workplace accessibility requirements, but there is no size limitation on the Title III requirements applicable to commercial facilities. Thus, even for very small businesses, accessibility requirements are imposed on new construction or alterations.

WHO IS RESPONSIBLE—LANDLORD OR TENANT?

Both the landlord and the tenant (the one who owns or operates a place of public accommodation) have responsibilities to remove barriers to accessibility, but neither the ADA nor the Equal Employment Opportunity Commission (EEOC) regulations on employment allocate these duties clearly. The responsibilities are not necessarily equal, and they may be allocated to the parties according to the lease.

If modifications of a physical structure are necessary as a reasonable accommodation for a disabled employee, the legal duty remains with the employer-tenant. If the rental agreement prohibits the tenant from making the modifications, the employer-tenant must make a good-faith effort to gain permission from the landlord. If the landlord refuses, what was a reasonable accommodation may become an undue hardship.

Existing leases are often unclear regarding each party's responsibilities. If a lease does not allocate responsibilities under the ADA, traditional legal principles would probably divide them as follows:

1. If the lease stipulates who is responsible for making alterations, the ADA's duty is on the named party. For example, if a lease between a physician and an office building owner specifies that no modifications may be made by the tenant, the duty is upon the landlord. The physician has a legal obligation to request that modifications be made to meet ADA requirements.

2. If the lease says that the tenant may not make alterations without the landlord's permission, the tenant must try to obtain permission. If the landlord refuses, the landlord may be liable for violation of the ADA.

If the landlord approves of the alterations but they are not completed, the tenant is in violation.

3. Generally, the tenant is responsible only for alterations in the *leased premises*, while the landlord is responsible for making readily achievable alterations in common areas such as the parking lot or building entrance. It remains the duty of the employer or business tenant to provide any required auxiliary devices that are not part of the leased structure.[1]

To avoid confusion about the respective duties of landlord and tenant, new leases should clearly establish each party's responsibilities for complying with the ADA. In this case, small business owners might want to have their legal counsel prepare a clause for rental contracts similar to that shown in Figure 7.1. The attorney may wish to add additional language concerning local and state requirements.

SPECIAL ACCESSIBILITY REQUIREMENTS FOR ENTITIES OFFERING TESTS AND COURSES

To ensure that key gateways to education and employment are open to people with disabilities, Title III of the ADA also requires any private entity that offers examinations or courses related to applications, licensing, certification, or credentialing to offer them in a place and manner accessible to persons with disabilities or to offer alternative accessible arrangements. A course might have to be offered on videocassette, or an examination might have to be given at an individual's home. The principles here are much the same as those governing preemployment screening discussed in Chapters 2 and 3. The examinations must reflect the individual's aptitude or achievement level rather than the individual's impairment. Examinations for individuals with disabilities must be offered as often as other examinations and at locations that are as convenient as those of other examinations.

Individuals requesting modifications or aids must provide advance notice and appropriate documentation. (This might include a letter from a physician or evidence of a prior diagnosis or accommodation.) The deadline for such notice cannot be any earlier than the deadline for

---

[1] James G. Frierson, *Employer's Guide to the Americans with Disabilities Act* (Washington, DC: The Bureau of National Affairs, 1992), 42.

Figure 7.1   Sample ADA Compliance Language for a Lease

The lessor (or landlord) promises and warrants that the leased offices, rooms, buildings, structures, and facilities covered by this rental or lease agreement comply with Title III of the Americans with Disabilities Act and the regulations issued thereunder by the United States Department of Justice concerning accessibility of places of public accommodation and commercial facilities. The lessor (or landlord) further promises and warrants that any common use areas or adjacent property owned or controlled by the lessor (or landlord) that might be used by employees, customers, clients, and the general public, such as parking lots, walkways, entrances, hallways, elevators, and other devices or pathways for egress and exit to the leased property, conform to the requirements of the Americans with Disabilities Act and all regulations issued thereunder by the Department of Justice or other authorized agencies under the authority of the Americans with Disabilities Act.

The lessor (or landlord) promises to reimburse and indemnify the lessee (or renter) for any expenses incurred because of the failure of the leased premises and adjacently owned property to conform to Title III of the Americans with Disabilities Act and the regulations issued thereunder, including the costs of making any alterations, renovations, or structural accommodations required under the Americans with Disabilities Act, or by any governmental enforcement agency or any court acting pursuant to Title III of the Americans with Disabilities Act. The lessor (or landlord) also promises to reimburse and indemnify the lessee (or tenant) for all fines, civil penalties, and violations of the above-cited law and regulations concerning the accessibility of commercial facilities and all reasonable legal expenses incurred in defending claims made under the above-cited law and regulations, including reasonable attorneys' fees.

Source: From p. 43 of the *Employer's Guide to the Americans with Disabilities Act* by James G. Frierson. Copyright © 1992, by The Bureau of National Affairs, Inc., Washington, DC 20037. Reprinted with permission.

others applying to take the test. The applicant may be required to bear the cost of providing the documentation, but the entity administering the examination cannot charge the applicant for any modifications or aids needed for the examination.

EMPLOYER DEFENSES

The "Readily Achievable" Standard

"Readily achievable" is not the same as "undue burden" or "undue hardship"—those two standards impose greater burdens upon employers and businesses. The readily achievable standard is easier to meet and was designed to prevent businesses from being forced into broadscale and costly modifications.[2] It means easily accomplishable and able to be carried out without much difficulty or expense. Relevant factors include:

- Nature and cost of removal.
- Financial resources of the facility, number of employees, effect on expenses and resources, and impact on operations.
- Financial resources of the overall company, its size, and the number of facilities it operates.
- The company's operations, the nature of the work force, geographic separateness, and administrative or fiscal relationship of the facilities to the parent company.

Costs

In general, costs will be an effective guide to determining whether an alteration is readily achievable. No magic cutoff number will provide a definite yes or no as to when a removal is readily achievable, because the size of the business is a significant factor. A $1,000 removal may be readily achievable for a large company but not for one that is smaller or less profitable.

One unanswered question in the law is whether a given alteration must be evaluated in isolation or along with similar alterations. For example, at a single facility or location, the widening of a door that

---

[2]Zachary Fasman, *What Business Must Know About the ADA: 1992 Compliance Guide* (Washington, DC: U.S. Chamber of Commerce, 1992), 61.

would cost $500 might seem to be readily achievable. But if there are 50 other doors that must be widened at a similar cost, the $25,000 total might far exceed the limited concept of readily achievable for that particular business, especially if the business is relatively small.

As with reasonable accommodation requests, the best approach probably would be to consider what is readily achievable in the context of each fiscal year, taking into account the priorities for barrier removal set forth in the Department of Justice regulations discussed earlier.

Examples _____

Retail stores may consider lowering their shelves to remove an architectural barrier to people in wheelchairs. However, it may not be readily achievable if it results in a significant loss of selling space. In this case, it might be more reasonable to try a different style of display rack or to have sales staff available to assist disabled customers.

ATM machines could be structurally lowered to be accessible to people in wheelchairs, but if this is not readily achievable an inexpensive ramp could be built to achieve the same result.

A public accommodation may not place a surcharge on an individual with a disability to cover the costs of providing auxiliary aids and services, removing barriers, or modifying policies and procedures. Likewise, charges may not be assessed for home delivery provided as an alternative to barrier removal unless home delivery is provided to all customers for a fee.

Fundamental Nature of the Business

You can justify a refusal to modify policies and procedures if the modifications would fundamentally alter the nature of the goods and services.

Example _____

A rehabilitation clinic that focuses on alcohol addiction would not have to treat an individual suffering from a drug dependency.

Undue Burden

Undue burden is a key concept in deciding whether a business is required to provide an auxiliary aid or service. The factors used to determine undue burden are essentially the same as those for the readily achievable standard or the undue hardship standard discussed in connection with Title I.

Following are some other points to consider in justifying a decision not to provide an auxiliary aid or service.

• ***Financial solvency of the company.*** Companies on the verge of bankruptcy may be able to demonstrate undue burden more readily than can healthy, profitable ones.

• ***Past efforts and expenditures.*** To the extent that you have already expended large sums in providing auxiliary aids and services or in removing barriers to equal access, additional expenditures may be more of a burden. On the other hand, what has proven reasonable for some disabilities could set the standard for the treatment of other conditions.

• ***Level of use.*** A very large expenditure for an aid that is not likely to be used much may be considered more of an undue burden. Keep in mind, though, that use of many auxiliary aids will be low because individuals with a given disability may not make up a significant percentage of the population. Use this defense carefully. If you can foresee that an aid is essential to the enjoyment of the service and would be used with at least some frequency, it should be provided.

• ***Costs and consequences to disabled people if auxiliary aid is not provided.*** The more serious the costs and results of denying an aid, the more difficult it becomes to show an undue burden.

• ***Administrative burden.*** In all likelihood, only administrative burdens that seriously threaten to disrupt the flow of services will be given any consideration. Inconveniences such as having to rearrange schedules probably will not go far in demonstrating an undue burden.

• ***Other industry efforts.*** To the extent that other comparable businesses in similar industries have provided auxiliary aids and services, it will be more difficult to show undue burden.[3]

---

[3]Fasman, *What Business Must Know About the ADA*, 58.

Public Safety

A business can justify allegedly discriminatory exclusion if it is necessary for safe operation of the business or if the individual's participation would pose a direct threat to the health or safety of others.

Example _____

A truck rental company might justify a requirement that all persons renting certain size trucks have a commercial vehicle license on the grounds of public safety.

On the other hand, the direct threat justification must establish that the risk to the health or safety of others cannot be eliminated by modifying policies and procedures or by providing auxiliary aids or services. The ADA prohibits safety-based exclusion of a broad class of individuals with no specific inquiry about the individual situation.

Department of Justice regulations specify that in determining whether an individual poses a direct threat, a business must conduct "an individualized assessment, based on a reasonable judgment that relies on current medical knowledge or on the best available objective evidence." Some safety concerns have no factual or medical foundation and are based upon the kinds of stereotypes the ADA seeks to eliminate.

Example _____

Fears about the risk of associating with an HIV-infected individual in a setting where there is no reasonable possibility of contracting the disease would not justify exclusion.

NEW CONSTRUCTION AND ALTERATIONS

For new construction and alterations or renovations of existing buildings, the ADA requires that the needs of individuals with disabilities be considered and that the resulting facility be "readily accessible to and usable by individuals with disabilities, including individuals who use wheelchairs." This applies both to commercial facilities, which include places of employment, and to public accommodations. This part of the ADA does not pertain to the construction or redesign of an individual workstation. That would fall under the Title I requirement for reasonable accommodation.

Also, in both new construction and alterations, businesses are not required to install elevators in facilities that are less than three stories high or that have less than 3,000 square feet per floor.

Alterations

The ADA's requirements for alterations apply only to alterations that are otherwise planned. A business does not have to undertake wholesale renovation of its facilities beyond the removal of the architectural and communication barriers discussed in the preceding chapter.

When alterations are made that affect the usability of areas of the facility containing a "primary function" of the business, to the maximum extent feasible, the path of travel to the altered area and to restrooms, telephones, and drinking fountains in that area also must be readily accessible and usable unless the cost of these alterations would be disproportionate to the overall alteration.

What Areas Contain a Primary Function? The law defines a primary function as "a major activity for which the facility is intended." The dining room of a cafeteria is an example of an area containing a primary function. A utility room in an office building probably would *not* be considered a primary function area. Justice Department regulations mention the following alterations as involving primary function areas:

- Remodeling merchandise display or employee work areas in a department store.
- Replacing an inaccessible floor surface in the customer service or employee work area of a bank.
- Redesigning the assembly line of a factory.
- Installing a computer center in an accounting firm.

What Is a Disproportionate Cost? According to Justice Department regulations, the cost of alterations will be considered disproportionate when it exceeds 20 percent of the cost of the alteration to the primary function area. The following may be counted as costs required to provide an accessible path of travel:

- Costs associated with providing an accessible entrance and an accessible route to the altered area.
- Costs associated with making restrooms accessible.
- Costs associated with providing accessible telephones.
- Costs associated with relocating an inaccessible drinking fountain or water cooler.

Where cost is disproportionate, the alteration may be made in another way. Even if the cost of full compliance is disproportionate, partial compliance is expected. In this case, alterations should be given priority in this order:

1. An accessible entrance.
2. An accessible route to the altered area.
3. At least one accessible restroom.
4. Accessible telephones.
5. Accessible parking, storage, and alarms.

Readily Accessible and Usable. This standard, which also applies to new construction, does not require that every part of a facility be accessible. It is generally applied to:

- Parking areas
- Routes to and from the facility
- Entrances
- Restrooms
- Water fountains
- Public use areas

A narrow exception to the accessibility requirement exists in situations in which it would be "structurally impracticable" to make a facility accessible because of the unique characteristics of the terrain, such as a building elevated on stilts in a flood or waterfront area.

New Construction

Although the new construction requirements became effective January 26, 1992, only new construction with first occupancy after January 26, 1993, is covered under the ADA. Justice Department regulations consider a facility to be designed and constructed for first occupancy after January 26, 1993, only if two conditions are met:

1. If the last application for a building permit or permit extension is completed after January 26, 1992.
2. If the first certificate for occupancy for the facility is issued after January 26, 1993.

This means that only facilities that are designed after January 26, 1992, and in which occupancy occurs after January 26, 1993, are covered by the ADA's requirements for new construction.

TITLE III REMEDIES AND ENFORCEMENT

Title III of the ADA is enforced through the remedies and procedures of Title II of the Civil Rights Act of 1964. Any person discriminated against in public accommodations or commercial facilities can do one of three things under the ADA:

- Sue for damages.
- File a complaint with the attorney general.
- Obtain an injunction through a federal district court to order that facilities be made readily accessible, that auxiliary aids or services be provided, that policies be modified, or that alternative methods be provided.

The attorney general has the authority to investigate Title III violations and to conduct compliance reviews to certify that state or local building codes comply with ADA accessibility guidelines. The law does not specify how these periodic reviews will be performed, but on-site inspections are most likely. The attorney general may bring or join a civil suit against persons engaged in a pattern and practice of discrimination and may sue on behalf of others in cases that present issues of general public importance.

The ADA prescribes a maximum civil penalty of $50,000 for the first violation and a maximum of $100,000 for subsequent violations. Punitive damages are not awarded, but attorney's fees are recoverable to prevailing parties under Title III. With respect to civil penalties, all good-faith efforts will be taken into consideration.

Even if an individual with a disability chooses not to accept an accommodation, he or she may still obtain remedies. Nothing in the act requires an individual with disabilities to accept any particular accommodation made on his or her behalf. The ADA encourages informal resolution of claims, but alternative methods such as mediation or arbitration are entirely voluntary. An individual can still file suit without exhausting these informal procedures.

CHAPTER EIGHT

ADA Accessibility Guidelines

On July 26, 1991, the Architectural and Transportation Barriers Compliance Board issued the Accessibility Guidelines for Buildings and Facilities (ADAAG) to implement Titles II and III of the Americans with Disabilities Act (ADA). In an attempt to coordinate the various private-sector and federal standards, the ADA guidelines are modeled on the widely used accessibility standards promulgated by the American National Standards Institute and the scoping provisions of the Council of American Building Officials' Board for the Coordination of Model Codes (BCMC).

STANDARDS FOR EXISTING BUILDINGS

Following is an overview of the ADA accessibility guidelines for making changes to existing buildings. By making a good-faith effort to follow these guidelines, you can make your facility more readily accessible to and usable by disabled individuals and perhaps safer all around. (See Figure 8.1 for a list of common barriers often found in existing buildings.)

Space Allowances for Wheelchairs

The minimum clear width for a single wheelchair passage is 32 inches. The minimum width for two wheelchairs to pass is 60 inches. The space

Figure 8.1   Identifying Common Barriers

Parking: Space is too narrow to permit transfer to wheelchair or crutches. Space is not level. A curb or step separates space from paved walk. Reserved sign is not visible.

Approach: Street between parking space and building entrance has no traffic light or curb cut at crossing. A step separates sidewalk and entrance level. Ramp is too steep for wheelchair.

Entrance: Doors are too narrow to admit wheelchair. Revolving doors operate while nearby swing doors are locked. Distance between outer and inner doors is too short. Excessive pressure is needed to operate doors.

Stairs: Steps have open risers or projecting nosings that can trip people using crutches. Handrail is too high or too low, or is difficult to grasp because of its size or shape.

Elevators: Entrance is too narrow to admit wheelchair. Door level is out of alignment with building floor. Controls for upper floors are out of reach. Buttons are flush, precluding unaided use by persons who are visually impaired. The audible arrival signal doesn't tell people whether cab is on the way up or down. Cab size is too small for wheelchair.

Floors: Floors between different parts of the building are not level and are connected by steps only. Floors are surfaced in slippery material or carpeted with deep-pile carpeting.

Restrooms: Restrooms on another floor are not connected by elevator. Double doors at entrance are situated so that wheelchair user must have both doors open at same time to pass through. Space is inadequate for turning wheelchair.

Water closet: Toilet stall door is too narrow to admit wheelchair. Door swings into the toilet stall. Stall has no grab bars. Water closet seat is too low or too high for transfer from wheelchair.

Lavatory: Clearance below bowl is too small to permit wheelchair to slide under. Hot water line is uninsulated. Towel bar, soap, and paper towel dispensers and disposal are out of reach. Mirror is out of line of vision.

Water fountain: Spout and controls are out of reach. Fountain is placed in alcove too narrow for wheelchair.

Coin-operated telephones: Telephone is set in a too-narrow enclosed booth. Coin slot, dial, and handset are out of reach. No amplification is available for persons who are hard of hearing.

Figure 8.1   *(Continued)*

Controls: Windows, draperies, heat and light controls, and fire alarms are situated out of reach of people in wheelchairs.

Hazards: Doors leading to boiler rooms and other hazardous spaces are not identifiable by touch. Floor access panels or holes are left unprotected. Paving has gratings that snag wheelchair wheels. Signs and fixtures are hung so low that they are a danger to persons with blindness.

Alarms: Fire alarms are audible only, without accompanying visual alarm for people with hearing impairments. Exit signs are not distinct enough to be distinguished by people with partial sight. Other typical barriers at the worksite include storage cabinets and shelves too high or too low; door swings that obstruct free movement of wheelchair; work bench or counter too low to permit wheelchair to slide under; no level station for wheelchair in auditorium; no existing auditorium seats removed to accommodate wheelchairs; aisles too narrow for wheelchairs; lockers inaccessible; cafeteria serving counters out of reach to people in wheelchairs; not enough leg clearance under restaurant tables.

Source: Reprinted with permission from *Employees Are Asking about Making the Workplace Accessible to Workers with Disabilities,* Washington, DC: President's Committee on Employment of People with Disabilities, 1991.

required for a wheelchair to make a 180-degree turn is a clear space 5 feet in diameter or 5 feet square to perform such activities as returning a tool to a bin or a book to a library shelf. The minimum clear floor space required to accommodate a stationary wheelchair and occupant is 30 by 48 inches. This could be considered "standing room" for performing job tasks such as operating a drill press or sorting mail. If the employee is seated in a wheelchair at a table or desk, then the free floor space underneath the work surface can be included in the above measurements.

When positioning time clocks, light switches, and electrical outlets, keep in mind that if the clear floor space allows a forward approach to an object, the maximum upward reach is 48 inches; the minimum low reach is 15 inches. If the clear floor space allows a parallel approach, the maximum upward reach is 54 inches and the low reach is no less than 9 inches above the floor.

Wheelchairs need a clear opening width of 32 inches to pass through doorways. Along corridors, aisles, tunnels, or other passageways, 36 inches is needed to accommodate the chair without scraping the occupant's hands against the side walls. If a passageway has less than 60 inches clear width, then passing spaces at least 60 inches by 60 inches must be located at 200-foot intervals.

Although people who use walking aids can maneuver through clear width openings of 32 inches, they need 36-inch-wide passageways and walks for comfortable gaits. Crutch tips, often extending down at a wide angle, are a hazard in narrow passageways where they might not be seen by other pedestrians. Thus, the 36-inch width provides a safety allowance both for the person with a disability and for others.

Accessible Routes

People with mobility impairments need an accessible path of travel extending from the nearest public transportation stop, adjacent parking lot, passenger drop-off point, or public sidewalk to a handicapped-accessible building entrance. This route should coincide with the route for the general public as closely as possible.

If an accessible route has changes in level greater than ½ inch, perhaps where two buildings were connected into one, then a ramp or platform lift must be installed. If the change in level is a story or more, a conventional elevator may be necessary.

In mapping out an accessible route, employers and business owners should be sensitive to the fact that many people with mobility impairments move very slowly; it could take two minutes to travel 200 feet— even longer if the person has to stop and rest. In inclement weather, slow progress can greatly increase a disabled person's exposure to the elements. Keep the accessible route as short as possible.

Curb Ramps

When an accessible route crosses a curb, such as at an intersection, the curb should have a ramp at least 36 inches wide. People with visual impairments can be alerted to the curb ramp's location, and to the danger of traffic, by a detectable warning built into the walking surface. Warning textures can be made in concrete ramps by scoring the surface, applying raised strips, or using a contrasting texture. Transitions from ramp to street must be flush and free of abrupt changes.

Parking and Passenger Loading Zones

Parking spaces for people with disabilities should be located on the shortest accessible route of travel from the parking lot to an accessible entrance. These parking spaces must be at least 96 inches wide, with an adjacent access aisle at least 60 inches wide to allow enough room for a wheelchair to pass between cars. Accessible parking spaces must be designated by a sign showing the international symbol of accessibility.

Entrances

Entrances must be connected by an accessible route to public transportation stops, to accessible parking and passenger-loading zones, and to public streets or sidewalks. They must also be connected by an accessible route to all accessible spaces within the building. A service entrance must not be the only accessible entrance.

Areas of Rescue Assistance

Because people with disabilities may visit or work in virtually any building, emergency management plans with specific provisions to ensure their safe evacuation play an essential role in fire safety. A 48-inch-wide exit stairway is needed to allowed assisted evacuation without encroaching on the path for ambulatory persons. Keep in mind that all accessible routes should comply with the egress requirements established by local fire codes and building authorities so that people with disabilities have an equal chance of evacuation. Emergency communication cannot depend on voice communications alone because the safety of people with hearing or speech impairments could be jeopardized. The visible signal requirement could be satisfied with something as simple as a button in the area of rescue assistance that lights to indicate that help is on the way.

Protruding Objects

It is important to keep not only floors free of obstacles, but the walls and ceilings as well. Fire extinguishers and wall-hung telephones could injure a person who is visually impaired. Any object that is mounted between 27 and 80 inches above the floor and protrudes more than 4 inches from the wall should be recessed. There is less threat of bumping into an object below 27 inches because a person walking with a cane can easily detect a protruding object at that height.

An individual who is visually impaired needs 80 inches of clear headroom in circulation areas. Water pipes, signs, fans, and other objects suspended from the ceiling should never descend below 80 inches into the path of travel. If they do, a guard rail or other detectable barrier should be installed to warn of the threat of striking one's head.

Floor Surfaces

Floor surfaces must be stable, firm, and slip resistant. If carpeting is used, it should have a firm, nonskid backing and a level texture with a pile height of no more than ½ inch. Exposed edges of area rugs must have a continuous trim and be fastened to the floor. If there are gratings in a floor surface, the spaces must be no more than ½ inch wide.

Ramps

Any part of an accessible route with a slope greater than 1 inch for each 20 feet of approach space must be considered a ramp. People who use wheelchairs have varying strengths in their arms and shoulders, so the least possible slope will suit the most people. The maximum slope of a ramp is 1:12. This means that if the vertical rise is 1 foot, the length of the ramp should be 12 feet. In an older building where space limitations prohibit the use of a 1:12 slope, a 1:8 slope may be used for a maximum rise of 3 inches.

The minimum clear width of a ramp is 36 inches. Ramps must have level landings of 60 inches clear at bottom and top. If a ramp makes a turn, a level 60-by-60-inch landing is required.

If a ramp run has a rise greater than 6 inches, it must have handrails on both sides. The handrails should be mounted between 30 inches and 34 inches above the surface of the ramp and protrude from the wall 1½ inches to allow room for gripping.

Ramps and landings with drop-offs must have curbs, walls, or railings to prevent people from slipping over the side. Outdoor ramps must be designed so that water will not accumulate on walking surfaces.

Stairs

All steps within a flight of stairs should have uniform riser heights and uniform tread widths. Treads should be no less than 11 inches wide from riser to riser. Open risers are not permitted. Stairways must have handrails at both sides of all stairs. The clear space between handrails and wall should be 1½ inches.

Elevators

People with disabilities should not have to use a freight elevator unless it is recognized and used by all employees or customers as a combination freight-passenger elevator. There are several points to consider in making an elevator convenient for people with disabilities. The car should be self-leveling and flush with floor landings. The call buttons in lobbies and halls should be placed 42 inches above the floor. The floor selection buttons in the elevator car should be no less than ¾ inch in their smallest dimension and have raised letters and numerals. If braille characters are used, they should be placed immediately to the left of the button to which they relate. Buttons should be no higher than 54 inches above the floor if there is room in the elevator for a wheelchair to make a parallel approach to the control panel, or 48 inches for a forward approach. A visible and audible signal should indicate when the car is arriving at a floor. Once the automatic doors open, there should be at least a 3-second delay before they begin to close.

Doors

A revolving door or turnstile cannot be the only means of passage. An alternative accessible doorway or gate must be provided for people who use wheelchairs, crutches, or canes. Doorways must have a minimum clear opening of 32 inches with the door open 90 degrees.

The minimum space between two doors in a series is 48 inches plus the width of any door swinging into the space. Doors in series must swing either in the same direction or away from the space between the doors.

Handles, latches, and other operating devices on accessible doors must have a shape that is easy to grasp with one hand and does not require tight gripping or twisting of the wrist to operate. Hardware should be mounted no higher than 48 inches above the finished floor. If a door has a closer, the timing must be adjusted so that the door will take at least 3 seconds to move from an open position of 70 degrees to a point 3 inches from the latch. The maximum allowable force for pushing or pulling open a door is about 5 pounds.

Drinking Fountains

Fountains and coolers can be used by a person from a wheelchair if the spout is no higher than 36 inches from the floor. The spout must be located at the front of the unit and must direct the flow of water parallel to the front of the unit. The water flow must be at least 4 inches high to allow a cup or glass to be inserted. Controls must be front mounted or side mounted near the front edge. Wall-mounted units need 27 inches of knee space underneath and at least 30 by 48 inches of clear floor space to allow a forward approach from a wheelchair. Freestanding units without knee space underneath can accommodate a parallel approach if they have the same clear floor space in front.

Signage

Characters and numbers on signs should be sized according to the viewing distance from which they are to be read. The minimum height is measured using an upper case X. Raised characters should be at least ⅝ inch high but no higher than 2 inches. Characters must contrast with their background—either light characters on a dark background or vice versa.

Signs that are permanently affixed to identify rooms should be installed on the wall adjacent to the latch side of the door if possible. Mounting height should be 60 inches above the floor to the centerline of the sign. A person should be able to approach to within 3 inches of the sign without encountering protruding objects or standing within the swing of a door.

Accessible facilities should be identified with the international symbol of accessibility or the international symbol of access for hearing loss.

Telephones

A wall-mounted public telephone should have at least 30 by 48 inches of clear floor space to allow for either a forward or parallel approach from a wheelchair. Bases and seats must not impede the approach. The highest operable part of the telephone must be between 48 and 54 inches, depending on the method of approach. Where possible, telephones must have pushbutton controls. The cord from the telephone to the handset must be at least 29 inches long.

If there is a bank of public telephones, such as in the lobby of an office building, then there should also be volume control equipment to accommodate people with hearing impairments. Some employers also provide telecommunications devices. Volume controls should range from a minimum of 12 decibels to a maximum of 18 decibels above normal.

Text telephones used with pay telephones must be permanently affixed within or adjacent to the telephone enclosure. If an acoustic coupler is used, the phone cord must be long enough to allow the text telephone to be hooked up to the telephone receiver. Pay telephones designed to accommodate a portable text telephone must be equipped with a shelf and an electrical outlet.

Restrooms

In making restrooms accessible, you have to take into consideration maneuvering space needed for wheelchairs, the size and arrangement of toilet stalls, the height of water closets and urinals, type of flush controls, and the placement of lavatories and mirrors. Following are some general guidelines from the ADAAG.

Toilet stalls. Toilet stalls generally have to be wider or deeper than conventional ones with enough room to transfer from a wheelchair to the toilet seat. The exact dimensions depend upon whether the water closet is wall mounted or on the floor, whether the stall door opens inward or outward, whether the partitions between stalls provide toe clearance of at least 9 inches, whether grab bars diminish the clear floor space, and whether the flush controls and toilet paper dispenser are within reach.

Water closets. Clear floor space may be arranged to allow either a left-handed or right-handed approach. The height of the water closet from the floor to the top of the toilet seat must be between 17 and 19 inches. Seats must not be sprung to return to a lifted position. The grab bar behind the water closet must be at least 36 inches long.

Urinals. Urinals can be stall type or wall hung at a maximum of 17 inches above the floor. If privacy shields are used, a clear floor space 30 by 48 inches must be provided in front of urinals to allow forward approach.

Lavatories and mirrors. Lavatories must be mounted with the rim or counter surface no higher than 34 inches above the floor and must provide a clearance of at least 29 inches above the floor to the bottom of the apron, with adequate knee and toe clearance. A clear floor space 30 by 48 inches must be provided in front of a lavatory to allow forward approach, and it must extend a maximum of 19 inches underneath the lavatory. Hot water and drain pipes under lavatories must be insulated or configured to protect against contact. There can be no sharp or abrasive surfaces under lavatories.

Mirrors should be mounted with the bottom edge of the reflecting surface no higher than 40 inches above the finish floor.

Storage Facilities and Operating Mechanisms

A clear floor space of at least 30 by 48 inches that allows either a forward or parallel approach must be provided at cabinets, shelves, closets, and drawers. Clothes rods or shelves must be no more than 54 inches above the floor for a side approach. Touch latches and U-shaped pulls are appropriate hardware for storage facilities. These specifications also apply to light switches, valves, blinds and drapery pulls, vending machine controls, and other operating mechanisms.

Seating

Seating at tables, counters, or work surfaces should have enough floor space and knee space to accommodate people in wheelchairs. The knee space must be at least 27 inches high, 30 inches wide, and 19 inches deep. The tops of tables and work surfaces should be from 28 to 34 inches from the floor. If possible, they should be adjustable so that they can be raised or lowered to meet individual needs.

Assembly Areas

When the seating capacity in assembly areas and company auditoriums exceeds 300, wheelchair spaces must be provided in more than one location. Wheelchair spaces must adjoin an accessible route that also serves as a means of egress in case of emergency. Readily removable seats may be installed in wheelchair spaces when the spaces are not needed to accommodate wheelchair users.

Alarms

To be effective, an emergency warning system should include both audible alarms for people who are visually impaired and visual alarms for those who are hearing impaired. The sound levels for audible alarms should not exceed 120 decibels, and flashing visual signals should have a frequency of about one flash per second.

Signs that provide emergency information or directions should use raised characters that can be felt by persons with visual impairments.

Hazard Warnings

People with visual impairments need a standardized system for identifying hazardous areas in a building. Detectable warnings on walking surfaces can be made by changing the texture of the surface or contrasting it with surrounding surfaces. Raised strips, grooves, cushioned surfaces, and roughened concrete are some ways to identify a path leading to a danger area. If a pedestrian walk or aisle crosses an area frequently used by vehicular traffic such as forklift trucks, some detachable warning should be used.

Doors that lead to boiler rooms, platforms, or any areas that might be dangerous should be identifiable to the touch by a textured surface on the door handle or other operating hardware. This can be done by knurling or roughening the knob or by applying tape to the contact surface.

STANDARDS FOR NEW CONSTRUCTION AND ALTERATIONS

Newly constructed buildings and buildings that are substantially altered or remodeled must adhere to the technical specifications outlined above. These buildings also have requirements governing the number of accessible entrances, parking spaces, telephones, seating, and the like that must be provided.

Elevators

Newly constructed office buildings that have less than three stories or less than 3,000 square feet per floor need not have elevator access to the upper floor. This means that a new two-story office building will not have to have an elevator even if each story has 20,000 square feet, nor would a five-story facility of 2,500 square feet per floor. The elevator exemption does not apply to shopping centers, shopping malls, or the professional offices of health care providers. These facilities must have elevators regardless of square footage or number of floors.

CHECKLIST FOR EVALUATING THE ACCESSIBILITY
OF YOUR FACILITY

Parking

- Are there spaces reserved for handicapped drivers?
- Is the space adequately marked with the international symbol of access?
- Is the accessible parking space as close as possible to an accessible building entrance (no more than 200 feet distance)?
- Is the parking space at least 8 feet wide, plus adjacent aisle space of 5 feet for a wheelchair to pass between cars?
- Is the route from the parking space to the accessible building entrance free of barriers such as curbs, steps, shrubbery, and fences?
- Is the number of spaces used by drivers who are disabled in accordance with the frequency and persistency of parking needs?

Ramps

- If a ramp is used to circumvent steps or other level changes, is it at least 36 inches wide?
- Is the slope or gradient of the ramp no more than a 1-foot rise in 12 feet?
- Are handrails on ramps between 30 and 34 inches high from the surface of the ramp?
- Do ramps have a nonslip surface?
- Do lengthy ramps have level platforms at 30-foot intervals and wherever the ramp turns for purposes of rest and safety?
- Does the ramp have level landings of 5-foot lengths at the top and bottom along the path of travel?

Entrance and Doorway

- Is there at least one primary entrance that is approached by a level or ramped walk?
- Is at least one entrance usable by individuals in wheelchairs on a floor accessible to the elevator?
- When the door is open, is there at least 32 inches of clear space for a wheelchair to pass through?

- Are the doors operable with pressure or strength that could reasonably be expected from a person with a disability?
- Is there an unobstructed level area inside and outside each doorway for at least 5 feet to allow a wheelchair to avoid the swing of the door?
- Is the threshold less than ½ inch high? Is it beveled?

Elevators

- In buildings taller than one story, are elevators available to people with disabilities?
- Does the elevator cab automatically come level with the lobby or corridor floor?
- Is the control panel installed so that the highest button is within 54 inches from the floor?
- Does the panel have raised symbols or numbers to permit persons who are visually impaired to select their floor?

Restrooms

- Do entry doors have a 32-inch clear opening?
- If there is a vestibule between two doors, is there a minimum space of 48 inches between the series of doors, not counting the width of any door swinging into the space?
- Do toilet rooms have enough turning space for people in wheelchairs?
- Is the height of the water closet between 17 and 19 inches when measured to the top of the toilet seat?
- Do lavatories have an underneath clearance of 29 inches measured from the floor?
- Are there grab bars fastened between 33 and 36 inches from the floor? Is there a 1½-inch space between the wall and the grab bar?
- Do toilet rooms have at least one toilet stall with a 32-inch-wide opening outward? Does the stall have a minimum depth of 56 inches and minimum width of 60 inches?
- Are drain pipes and hot water pipes covered or insulated?
- Are mirrors mounted with the bottom edge no higher than 40 inches from the floor?

Drinking Fountains

- Is the spout of the fountain no higher than 36 inches from the floor?

- Are the spout and the controls near the front of the unit?
- With cantilevered units, is there knee clearance between the bottom of the fountain and the floor? Do freestanding units without clear space under them have floor space in front at least 30 by 48 inches to allow for parallel approach in a wheelchair?

Public Telephones

- If public telephones are provided, are the highest operable parts no higher than 54 inches from the floor?
- Are telephones available that are equipped for persons with hearing impairments? Are they identified as such?
- Is there a clear floor space at each accessible public telephone of at least 30 inches by 48 inches?

Work Surfaces

- Are the tops of tables and work surfaces 28 to 34 inches from the floor? Different types of work require different surface heights for comfort and performance. Writing, for instance, requires a higher work surface than manual work.

Alarms

- Does the emergency warning system include both audible and visual alarms?

Warning Signals

- Are there walking surfaces textured to indicate approaching hazardous areas such as tops of stairs?
- Are there tactile warnings on doors to hazardous areas such as loading platforms, boiler rooms, or fire escapes?

Signage

- Is the international symbol of access used to indicate general circulation directions or identify rooms and spaces that are accessible to people with disabilities?

Source: Lotito, Michael, et al. *Making the ADA Work for You,* 2d ed. Northridge, Calif.: Milt Wright & Associates, 1992, pp. 61–64. Reprinted with permission.

Parking

The number of accessible parking spaces should be provided in accordance with Table 8.1.

Entrances

Because entrances also serve as emergency exits, it is best that *all* entrances be accessible. In terms of the ADA's new construction requirements, however, at least 50 percent of all public entrances must be accessible and at least one must be a ground floor entrance. (This does not include loading or service entrances.) An accessible entrance must be provided to each tenant in a facility (for example, to individual stores in a strip shopping center). If possible, accessible entrances should be the ones used by most people visiting or working in the building.

The number of accessible entrances must be equivalent to the number of exits required by the building fire codes. This does not require an increase in the total number of entrances planned for a facility.

If direct access is provided for pedestrians from an enclosed parking garage to the building, at least one direct entrance from the garage to the building must be accessible. The same applies to tunnels and pedestrian walkways.

Assembly Areas

In places of assembly with fixed seating, accessible wheelchair locations must be provided consistent with the ratio shown in Table 8.2.

Table 8.1   Required Number of Accessible Parking Spaces

Total Parking Spaces in Lot	Required Number of Accessible Spaces
1 to 25	1
26 to 50	2
51 to 75	3
76 to 100	4
101 to 150	5
151 to 200	6
201 to 300	7

Table 8.2   Required Number of Wheelchair Locations in Assembly Areas

Seating Capacity in Assembly Area	Number of Required Wheelchair Locations
4 to 25	1
26 to 50	2
51 to 300	4
301 to 500	6
over 500	6 plus 1 space for each 100 seats

In addition, 1 percent, but not less than one, of all fixed seats must be aisle seats with no armrests, or with folding armrests, on the aisle side. Accessible seats should be identified by a sign or marker.

Drinking Fountains

Where there is more than one drinking fountain or water cooler on a floor, 50 percent of them must be wheelchair accessible and located on an accessible route.

Where only one drinking fountain is provided on a floor, there should be a drinking fountain that is accessible to people who use wheelchairs and one that is at a standard height for those who have difficulty bending or stooping. This can be accommodated by the use of a "hi-lo" fountain.

Telephones

If public telephones are provided, then a certain number of them must be wheelchair accessible, hearing aid-compatible, and equipped with a volume control (see Table 8.3).

In addition, 25 percent, but never less than one, of all other public telephones provided must be equipped with a volume control. If four or more public pay phones (both interior and exterior) are provided, at least one interior public text telephone must be provided.

Where a bank of telephones in the interior of a building consists of three or more public pay phones, at least one telephone in each bank must be equipped with a shelf and an outlet to accommodate a portable text telephone.

Table 8.3   Acquired Number of Accessible and Specially Equipped Telephones

Number of Phones on Each Floor	Number of Accessible and Specially Equipped Phones
1 or more single units	1 per floor
1 bank*	1 per floor
2 or more banks	1 per bank

*A bank is two or more adjacent phones.

Built-In Tables and Seating

If fixed or built-in seating or tables (as in student laboratory stations or library study carrels) are provided in public or common use areas, at least 5 percent, but not less than one, of the seats or tables must be wheelchair accessible. An accessible route must lead to and through the accessible seating area.

CHAPTER NINE

Accommodating Specific Disabilities

Let's look at how some businesses have dealt with major limiting conditions that cut across a variety of functions: lifting and carrying, sitting, manual tasks, mobility, hearing, and seeing. We shall also consider employment of mentally retarded workers.[1]

LIFTING AND CARRYING

No job is completely free from lifting or carrying tasks, yet these tasks can cause problems for people with heart conditions, spinal cord injuries, cerebral palsy, or limited stamina. One of the most common reasons for difficulty in lifting or carrying is injury to the lower back, an injury that affects some 80 percent of the American population. It has been estimated that low back pain costs between $20 million and $30 million in worker's compensation costs and lost productivity.

---

[1]Except as noted, information in this chapter has been adapted from Michael Lotito, et al., *Making the ADA Work for You*, 2d ed. (Northridge, Calif.: Milt Wright & Associates, 1992), pp. 71–88. Reprinted with permission.

The following guidelines for job modifications can help to prevent back injuries and minimize their limitations.[2]

Problems and Solutions

1. Objects are too large or too heavy.
   - Assign the task to more than one worker.
   - Distribute the load into more than one container.
   - Use assistive equipment such as carts or overhead cranes.
   - Modify the tasks.
   - Provide handles or hooks to assure a firm grip on objects.
   - Provide smooth surfaces to permit sliding rather than lifting.
   - Use lightweight containers; change container shape.
   - Use large-wheeled carts to minimize effort.
2. Objects are not accessible.
   - Where possible, locate objects from 20 to 52 inches above floor.
   - Provide height-adjustable work surfaces, storage, and seating.
   - For object assembly, ensure access to all sides of worktable; use turntables if necessary.
   - Locate objects at level to which they must be lifted.
   - Minimize reaching into deep storage containers through use of spring-loaded or sloped bottoms.
3. Frequency or duration of lifting/carrying causes fatigue.
   - Allow more time to complete task.
   - Reduce frequency of task.
   - Rotate workers to limit exposure to stress.
   - Provide rest periods.
   - Control temperature extremes.

Scenario

In a television repair shop, a worker with limited strength in his legs had to regularly lift television sets from the floor to his worktable and then back down onto the floor for removal. Because each technician at this shop works independently, asking a coworker to help would disrupt overall productivity. As an alternative, the company purchased a free-

---

[2]M. A. Ayoub, "Control of Manual Lifting Hazards. II. Job Redesign," *The Journal of Occupational Medicine* 24 (Sept. 1982):668–676.

standing electronic platform lift that would raise and lower the sets for him. The device cost approximately $450.

SITTING

Seating accommodations should take into account the nature of the disability (e.g., paralysis, arthritis, hip injury) as well as the job itself. Because seating determines posture and movement patterns, a well-designed chair can even prevent disabilities. Studies indicate that a good chair can add up to 40 minutes of production to a workday. The mechanics of sitting include awareness of balance, hip and leg pressure, and alignment of the vertebral column. The preferred solution among ergonomics professionals is a fully adjustable chair.

The following job design guidelines can help to prevent physical problems and maximize productivity in the workplace.

Problem and Solutions

Employee complains of excessive fatigue at the end of the workday.

- Seating should allow the user's feet to either touch the floor or a footrest on the chair. The seat should be height adjustable to between 14 and 20 inches above the floor.
- The backrest on the chair should be adjustable for both angle and height to provide appropriate lumbar support.

Scenario

A copy machine operator with arthritis was having difficulty reaching up and across the machine to perform certain tasks. Because the machine was too complex to alter, the operator's working height was changed with a height-adjustable stool. The stool provided full back support and a platform for her feet. It cost about $350.

MANUAL TASKS

Poorly designed work patterns, vibration, and repetitive hand motions can contribute to chronic hand, arm, shoulder, and back problems. Job task analyses, time-and-motion studies, and equipment inspections can help an employer determine what accommodations will be most productive for workers who have trouble performing manual tasks.

The following modification guidelines illustrate different ways in which an employer can enable people with manual limitations to continue on the job.

Problems and Solutions

1. Task is too complex.
    *   Store tools and equipment for a particular task in one place.
    *   Change task sequences to increase efficiency.
    *   Provide assistive devices where needed.
    *   Eliminate nonessential movements; combine essential movements.
2. Worker doesn't have sufficient hand and forearm strength to operate tools.
    *   Suspend or counterbalance heavy tools.
    *   Provide tools that can be used in either hand.
    *   For single-hand tools, grip span should be between 2 and 4 inches.
    *   Design hand tools for operation with a straight wrist. The rule is "bend the tool, not the wrist."[3]
3. Severely disabled workers cannot perform certain manual tasks.
    *   Provide electronic equipment with voice or touch control devices.
    *   Install electric tools.

Scenario

A manufacturing assembler complained of chronic carpal tunnel syndrome in his wrists and hands. A thorough job analysis revealed that repeated reaching for parts in boxes created constant wrist-bending demands on the worker. The workstation was redesigned with shallow bins so that parts could be stored on each side of the worker and at table height. The individual was encouraged to take breaks at regular intervals. A $100 job accommodation for the new bins improved the worker's productivity and decreased sick leave.

---

[3]Problems 1 and 2 were adapted from T. Armstrong, *Ergonomics Guides: An Ergonomic Guide to Carpal Tunnel Syndrome.* (Akron, Ohio: American Industrial Hygiene Association, 1983).

MOBILITY

Mobility in the workplace must take into account all areas related to work, including the parking lot, restrooms, cafeteria, and workstations. It is a good idea to involve employees in planning mobility accommodations.

Following are some general guidelines for accommodating people with mobility impairments.

Problems and Solutions

1. Common areas and pathways to work site need to be made more accessible.
   • Parking spaces near the building should be reserved for people with disabilities; spaces should be at least 13 feet wide to allow for wheelchairs or van lifts.
   • Entrance doors should have a clear opening of 32 inches (36 inches in some states); use accessible door hardware.
   • Ramps or lifts may be needed to negotiate changes in floor level.
2. The work site is inconvenient for disabled workers.
   • Make all storage and shelving accessible from a seated position.
   • Provide storage for crutches, walkers, and canes.

Scenario

On evaluating the work site of a secretary in a wheelchair, it was observed that the calculator was located on a coworker's desk and the computer terminal was at yet another workstation. Maneuvering the wheelchair between the desks was difficult, so the employer organized the equipment on a turntable at the secretary's workstation. This made her more efficient, and it removed the safety hazard from cords draped across the floor. The turntable cost about $400.

HEARING

There are 15 to 20 million hearing-impaired people in the United States. Between 350,000 and 2 million of them are totally deaf. Major modifications to the work area are not usually necessary to accommodate hearing-impaired workers or job applicants. Most people who became deaf later in life can speak, and many deaf people use a combination of speech, sign language, and lip-reading. For the most part, communicating with them is a matter of sensitivity and common sense.

Accommodation Ideas

• Train immediate coworkers in American Sign Language. The basics can be learned in a few hours, so the expense is minimal. Some local organizations provide sign language classes.

• Designate another employee or ask for volunteers to keep the hearing-impaired employee aware of informal communications such as the office "grapevine" and to alert the person in an emergency.

• Use signaling devices such as a flashing light for customer service or a telephone flasher that signals when the phone rings.

• Provide vibrating pagers to contact deaf employees in the field.

• Minimize vibrations in the work area. They distort sounds received by a hearing aid.

• Use sound amplification devices (volume control, high-intensity ring) on telephones.

• Install telecommunication devices for the deaf (TDDs).

More than 100,000 TDDs are in use today. In the past, these devices could be used only if the person on the other end of the phone call also had a TDD to receive the printed message. The Americans with Disabilities Act eliminates this restriction by requiring telephone companies to provide relay services whereby a deaf person can use a TDD or type a message that is converted by the phone company into an audible form. Similarly, voice communications to a deaf recipient are relayed from voice to TDD. TDDs cost from $150 to about $1,000, depending upon the brand and the number of options you add.

Scenario

A federal agency accommodated a deaf distribution clerk who was asked the same routine questions by other employees by providing six question signs that the hearing employees could use to indicate their questions and 12 preprinted cards that the deaf employee could use in answering.

SEEING

Some 14 million Americans are visually impaired, which is defined as unable to read regular-size print, even with glasses. About 800,000 people are legally blind, which means that even with glasses they can see something at 20 feet no better than someone with normal sight can see at 200 feet. It is estimated that more than 80 percent of the 32,000 jobs listed in the *Dictionary of Occupational Titles* can be performed by visually-impaired persons with proper job analysis, training, and equipment. Nevertheless, studies show that 70 percent of the working-age people with serious vision problems are unemployed or underemployed.

People who have trouble seeing can't rely on visual cues. They need environmental cues to help them navigate around the workplace. Lights, strong colors, or red markers can help locate machine controls, mechanical tools, stair treads, light switches, and door knobs. Consistent location of furniture and equipment can map the path of travel.

Following are examples of the many tools and devices on the market that make it possible for people with visual impairments to accomplish almost any task.

Electronic Aids (approximate prices)

- Safety saw guide for blind carpenters (under $25).
- Talking calculator (under $40).
- Telephone that stores up to 200 names and phone numbers and automatically dials a number upon a spoken command (under $200).
- Braille printer for computer ($1,000).
- Computer voice commands that work with most word-processing programs ($250).
- Talking lap computer with braille command system (under $3,000).
- Braille pocket folding tape measure ($13).
- Various "talking" measuring tools ($150 to $500).
- Illuminated magnifiers ($20 to $50).
- Portable print enlarger ($950 to $1,800).
- Enlarged numbers that fit over a touchtone phone (under $15).

- Combination lamp and magnifying glass ($35).
- Voice-recognition system that allows one to convert spoken commands into 64 different computer commands ($150).

Administrative Accommodations

- ***Physical orientation.*** A blind or visually-impaired person needs help in becoming oriented to the workplace. The new employee should be taken around the office, sales floor, assembly line, or other place of work. Everything should be described in detail. The person should be walked through the premises so that he or she can move freely around the workplace to entrances, exits, and restrooms. The location of tools and office supplies should be pointed out and the employee should be encouraged to touch objects to orient their location.

- ***Employee education.*** Supervisors and coworkers should be informed of the new employee's needs and qualifications before the person begins work. It will be much easier to enlist their cooperation if they understand the situation in advance. However, if the vision problem is not obvious, coworkers should not be informed until after the person has voluntarily disclosed the problem.

Scenario

A blind machinist's job involved machining parts for hydraulic cylinders. For under $300, she was provided with a braille micrometer to measure the diameter of precision metal shafts.

A DuPont employee who lost his sight from an optic nerve tumor was able to return to his job as a computer programmer thanks to a voice synthesizer that allowed his computer to talk. The cost was under $1,000.

MENTAL RETARDATION

Some 6 million Americans are mentally retarded. More than 90 percent of them are only mildly retarded (an IQ of 51 to 70) and can perform all types of work without anyone recognizing their retardation. Those who are considered severely retarded cannot generally work in a competitive environment, but they have been employed successfully in sheltered workshops and in "enclaves" within private companies. Enclave workers are placed in a special area of the company under a trained supervisor, usually to do simple, repetitive work.

There is no connection between retardation and mental illness. Mentally retarded people simply learn more slowly. Although retarded people may take longer to master a job, once they do learn it they are not slower in performing.[4]

Some people feel that retarded workers should not be mixed with other workers. Although retarded people may be slow to socialize with coworkers, experience has shown that they generally work side by side with nondisabled employees without difficulty. With adequate training, a retarded worker should not require any extra supervision. As with all employees, supervisors must be sensitive and straightforward in dealing with them.

Various public and private organizations can assist in training mentally retarded workers. Some can offer financial support; others may furnish a job coach to work with the retarded person for the first few weeks. Tax deductions and credits are also possible, as discussed in Chapter 6.

Scenario

As reported in *The New York Times*,[5] the owner of a commercial laundry in Russellville, Arkansas, found it hard to find people who would start at the minimum wage. He began recruiting workers from the Russell Skills Center, a local sheltered workshop for people who are retarded and have other mental disabilities, to do folding, sorting, and processing of laundry. Today, 5 of the company's 16 employees come from the center. The agency provides coaches for the workers until they learn their routines.

To keep up production, Kreonite, the Wichita-based manufacturing company mentioned in the Introduction to this book, recently brought in a team of mentally disabled workers from a local sheltered workshop, the Kansas Elks Training Center for the Handicapped. With about 15 percent of its 240-member work force consisting of people with disabilities, Kreonite employs a full-time disability coordinator to supervise these workers. The company's senior vice-president maintains that workers, disabled or not, need supervisors. Kreonite just employs one who is skilled in dealing with disabilities.

---

[4]James G. Frierson, *Employer's Guide to the Americans with Disabilities Act* (Washington, DC: The Bureau of National Affairs, 1992), 329.
[5]Peter Kilborn, "Major Shift Likely as Law Bans Bias Toward Disabled." *The New York Times*, 19 July 1992, sec. 1.

CHAPTER TEN

Some Common Questions and Answers about the ADA

Under what circumstances can an employer establish physical criteria for a job position?
An employer can apply any criterion that is job related and consistent with business necessity. If lifting 50-pound boxes is essential to a particular job, an employer can require that an applicant for that position be able to lift 50 pounds. If the person could perform the lifting with a reasonable accommodation, the employer may not deny that individual the job.

Does an employer violate the Americans with Disabilities Act (ADA) by hiring an applicant who does not have a disability if that person is more qualified than a disabled applicant?
No. An employer may hire an applicant who does not have a disability if that person is more qualified for the job in question as long as the determination was not based on criteria that discriminate on the basis of disability.

The employer may not use an applicant's ability to perform nones-

---

Note: Excerpted in part from *Task Force Report on the Americans with Disabilities Act*, prepared by Littler, Mendelson, Fastiff & Tichy, 1991.

tial functions of the job as part of the selection process. If answering the phone were not an essential function of a typist's job, an employer could not, on that basis, choose a hearing applicant over an applicant who is deaf if both were equally qualified to perform the essential job functions.

Is it a legitimate defense to refuse to hire someone whose disability would pose a threat to the safety of others?
Yes. The ADA stipulates that a legitimate qualification standard is that a person not pose a "direct threat to the health or safety of others in the workplace." The term *direct threat* is defined as a "significant risk that cannot be eliminated by reasonable accommodation."

As part of the job application process at some companies, applicants are required to undergo a medical examination. Is this still permitted under the ADA?
An employer cannot ask a job applicant whether he or she has a disability. An employer may require a medical examination only *after* an offer of employment is made and *before* the applicant starts the job. The offer of employment may be conditioned on the results of the examination.

Because information about an applicant's medical condition must be treated as confidential, how can management be told what steps to take to accommodate a disabled person?
The ADA provides that supervisors and managers may be informed of any restrictions on the duties of the employee and any accommodations that are necessary for him or her to perform the job. The employer also may inform first-aid or safety personnel and government officials who are investigating violations of the act.

Can a company test employees or applicants for drugs?
The ADA places no restrictions on drug testing of applicants or employees, as long as the tests are designed to identify illegal drugs.

Is a personnel policy that prohibits illegal use of drugs and alcohol at the company still acceptable under the ADA?
An employer may require that employees not be under the influence of alcohol or engage in the illegal use of drugs at the workplace. The ADA is not meant in any to undercut the requirements established under the Drug Free Workplace Act of 1988.

If state law provides protection for individuals with disabilities different from those covered by the ADA, which law would apply?
The ADA does not invalidate or limit state laws that provide greater or equal protection to individuals with disabilities.

Can an employer refuse a job to a person with a disability because the company's insurance plan does not cover the particular person's disability or because of an anticipated increase in insurance costs?
No. This would be a violation of section 501 (c) of the ADA.

Can insurance companies or employers deny health insurance coverage to an individual based solely on the person's diagnosis or disability?
No. All people with disabilities must have equal access to the health insurance coverage that the employer provides to all employees. A limitation may be placed on reimbursement for a procedure or the types of drugs or procedures covered, but that limitation must apply to persons with or without disabilities.

Can insurance companies or employers continue plans that limit certain kinds of coverage based on classification or risk?
Yes. However, an insurer may not refuse to continue to insure an individual or charge a different rate for the same coverage where the refusal or limitation is not based on sound actuarial principles or related to reasonable anticipated experience. Employers may continue to offer policies that contain preexisting condition exclusions even though such exclusions adversely affect people with disabilities, so long as such clauses are not used as a subterfuge to evade the purpose of this legislation. Similarly, while an insurer can deny coverage for an existing condition for a time, the coverage may not be denied for illnesses unrelated to the preexisting condition.

Is an overweight person covered by the ADA?
Probably not. Being overweight is simply a physical characteristic. However, some individuals may be so obese that it is a recognizable physiological disorder. It might, for instance, interfere with their breathing. These individuals would be covered under the ADA.

Does the ADA cover people with AIDS?
Yes. Under the ADA, a person suffering from a contagious disease is considered disabled. This includes people with AIDS and those who test positive for HIV.

Would a person who was not hired because he or she wore glasses be covered?
Yes. A person wears glasses to compensate for a visual impairment. This physiological disorder substantially limits the major life activity of seeing, even though the disorder may be corrected through the use of glasses.

An employee has a broken arm and is temporarily unable to perform the essential functions of his job as a machinist. Is he protected by the ADA?
No. Although this employee does have an impairment, it does not substantially limit a major life activity if it is of limited duration and will have no long-term effect.

Is a pregnant employee protected under the ADA?
Pregnancy is one of several conditions that are excluded from ADA protection. Others include: homosexuality, bisexuality, transvestitism, pedophilia, voyeurism, compulsive gambling, kleptomania, and pyromania.

Will I have to make changes in the workstation to accommodate left-handed employees?
No. Simple physical traits such as left-handedness, blue eyes, or black hair do not constitute impairments under the ADA.

What is job restructuring?
Job restructuring refers to modifying a job so that a person with a disability can perform the central functions of the position. Barriers to performance may be removed by eliminating nonessential elements of the job, redelegating assignments, exchanging assignments with another employee, and redesigning procedures. The key to job restructuring is flexibility.

Must an employer bump another employee out of a position to accommodate a disabled person?
No. It is clear that the reassignment need only be to a vacant position. Bumping another employee out of a position to create a vacancy is not required.

Is a collective bargaining agreement relevant in determining whether a given accommodation is reasonable?
Yes. If a collective bargaining agreement reserves certain jobs for employees with a given amount of seniority, it may be considered as a factor in determining whether it is a reasonable accommodation to assign an employee with a disability without seniority to the job.

What if an applicant or employee refuses to accept an accommodation that I offer?
The ADA provides that an employer cannot require a qualified individual with a disability to accept an accommodation that is not requested or needed. However, if a necessary, reasonable accommodation is refused, the individual may be considered not qualified.

Who has responsibility for removing barriers in a shopping mall, the landlord who owns the property or the tenant who leases the store?
Both landlord and tenant have responsibilities unless a clearly defined agreement is in place. In most cases, the landlord will have full control over common areas.

If our business has a fitness room for its employees, must it be accessible to employees with disabilities?
Yes. Under the ADA, workers with disabilities must have equal access to all benefits and privileges of employment. The duty to provide reasonable accommodation applies to all nonwork facilities that you provide for your employees—cafeterias, lounges, auditoriums, transportation, and counseling services.

If I contract with a consulting firm to develop a training course for my employees and the firm arranges for the course to be held at a hotel that is inaccessible to one of my employees, am I liable under the ADA?
Yes. An employer may not do through a third-party what it is prohibited from doing directly. You would have to provide a site that is readily accessible to the employee with a disability unless doing so would create an undue hardship.

How does the ADA recognize public health concerns?
The ADA recognizes the need to strike a balance between the right of a disabled person to participate in the mainstream of American life and the right of the public to be protected from legitimate health threats. The ADA is not intended to supplant the role of public health authorities in protecting the community.

Does the ADA cover private apartments and private homes?
The ADA generally does not cover private residential facilities. These are covered in the Fair Housing Amendments Act of 1988, which prohibits discrimination on the basis of disability in selling or renting housing. If a building contains both residential and nonresidential portions, only the nonresidential portions are covered by the ADA. In a large hotel with a residential apartment wing, the residential units would be covered by the Fair Housing Act and the other rooms would be covered by the ADA.

Will businesses need to install elevators?
Businesses are not required to retrofit their facilities to install elevators unless such installation is readily achievable. Even in new buildings, elevators are not required in structures under three stories or with less

than 3,000 square feet of space per floor unless the building is a shopping center or professional office of a health care provider.

What does the term *readily achievable* mean?
It means "easily accomplishable and able to be carried out without much difficulty or expense."

What are examples of the types of modifications that would be readily achievable?
Examples include ramping of steps, the installation of grab bars, and lowering of telephones.

How is "readily achievable" determined in a multi-site business?
In determining whether an action to make a public accommodation accessible would be "readily achievable," the overall size of the parent corporation or entity is only one factor to be considered. The ADA also looks at the financial resources of the particular facility involved and the administrative or fiscal relationship of the facility to the parent entity.

Will restaurants be required to have braille menus?
No, not if waiters or other employees are made available to read the menu to a visually-impaired customer.

Will businesses need to rearrange furniture and display racks?
Possibly. Restaurants may need to rearrange tables, and department stores may need to adjust their layout of racks and shelves to permit wheelchair access.

If I hire someone with a disability and it doesn't work out, can I dismiss the person without charges being filed?
No one can ever be sure whether charges will be filed for dismissal. However, the ADA does not force employers to keep incompetent or unproductive employees. It is important, though, to document the reasons for dismissal.

Is an employee who is injured on the job protected by the ADA?
An injury and a disability are not necessarily the same thing. Whether an injured worker is protected by the ADA will depend on whether or not the person meets the ADA definition of a "qualified individual with a disability." The person's injury must substantially limit a major life activity. A worker who can no longer perform the essential functions of the job with or without an accommodation must be considered for a

vacant position at the same or lower grade level for which he or she is qualified.

The fact that an employee is awarded worker's compensation benefits does not automatically establish that this person is protected by the ADA because many work-related injuries are not severe enough or long-term enough to substantially limit a major life activity. The definition of a disability under most state laws differs from the ADA's. State worker's compensation laws are designed to assist workers who suffer many kinds of injuries, whereas the ADA is meant to protect people from discrimination on the basis of a disability.

What if an employee lies about his or her physical condition?
An employer can fire or refuse to hire a person who knowingly provides a false answer to a lawful postoffer inquiry about his or her condition or worker's compensation history.

Some state laws release an employer from its obligation to pay worker's compensation benefits if an employee misrepresents his or her physical condition when hired and is later injured as a result.

What should an employer do when a worker is injured on the job?
If the worker's injury appears to affect his or her ability to perform the essential functions of the job, a medical examination or inquiry would be consistent with business necessity. It might also be necessary to provide reasonable accommodation. When an employee wishes to return to work after an accident or illness, the employer can require only a *job-related* medical examination, not a complete physical, as a condition of returning to work.

An employer cannot refuse to let an individual with a disability return to work because the worker is not fully recovered unless he or she cannot perform the essential functions of the job with or without reasonable accommodation or would pose a significant risk of substantial harm to him-or herself or others.

Can a person file a discrimination charge against an employer on more than one basis?
Yes. A visually-impaired woman worker can claim that she was discriminated against on the basis of both her sex and her disability. She can file a single charge alleging both forms of discrimination.

Situation
Analyses

Situation No. 1

An applicant sends a resumé in response to a help wanted ad for a draftsperson. The resumé indicates that she has a "speech impediment." The employer calls her to schedule an interview and asks whether the impediment is more severe when she is under pressure at work.

Can the employer ask this question? If so, must the employer accept the applicant's reply to determine if she is qualified for the job?

Analysis. No and NO!

The Americans with Disabilities Act (ADA) doesn't prevent employers from obtaining medical and related information about an applicant's ability to perform essential job functions. However, three things are very wrong with this picture:

1. No such inquiry can be made before a job offer is extended. Here, there was not even an interview.
2. The inquiry must concern ability to perform *essential* job functions; "normal" speech bears no relationship to drafting skill.
3. The applicant's reply has nothing to do with her objective qualifications to perform the job.

Situation No. 2

An applicant has been medically diagnosed as HIV positive. He explains this to the employer during the interview. The employer is impressed with the applicant's background, qualifications, and personality. However, hiring the applicant is sure to result in other employees quitting and filing worker's compensation stress claims.

What can the employer do?

Analysis. Technically, nothing can be done. Any rejection of the applicant must be justified by: (1) An objective risk of (2) substantial harm, (3) documented by medical or other proof, and (4) evidence that it can't be reduced or eliminated by a (5) reasonable accommodation to the applicant.

As a practical matter, this employer can probably avoid hiring the applicant though. Because no offer was extended, legality yields to practicality—and morality.

Situation No. 3

An applicant has a history of excessive absenteeism because of chronic fatigue. He is applying for a position as a night security guard. The employer extends an offer conditioned upon passing a preemployment physical examination. No other applicants were examined prior to being hired.

Can the physical exam be a condition of employment?

Analysis. Yes and no.

An offer of employment can be conditioned upon passage of a preemployment physical exam. A preemployment physical can also be required selectively for some jobs and not for others.

However, it can't be done for some employees in similar jobs and not for others. The actual job title doesn't matter—a day security guard should probably be required to take the same physical exam.

If the same degree of mental and physical alertness is not necessary, some difference in the requirements might be justified.

Situation No. 4

After extending an offer, the employer checks the state worker's compensation records. He discovers that the applicant filed four claims over the past five years, and three were denied. The employer suspects the claims were fraudulent.

The employer withdraws the offer of employment, telling the applicant he no longer needs to fill the job opening.

Can he do so?

Analysis. Probably.

The employer can definitely reject the applicant without incurring liability under the ADA.

This is not a decision based on disability. It is based on a suspicion of fraudulent claims and the likelihood that the employer will be the next victim. There is no liability for misrepesenting the reason for not hiring, either. The employer is under no specific duty to give the real reason.

Even if the employer hires someone else for the same job, the applicant would have difficulty establishing a vested right to it.

Situation No. 5

After an applicant is hired, the preemployment physical examination reveals that she would need medical treatment over a six-month period. She is a highly qualified engineer, but would require three weeks of intermittent absence. However, scheduling of a major project requires her daily attendance.

Can the offer be revoked?

Analysis. Yes.

She is not available to perform the job, and no accommodation is possible.

This is an example of the difference between a rejection based on disability and one based on absenteeism.

Accommodation of a disability can be balanced against business necessity.

Situation No. 6

After receiving an offer, an applicant submits a prior medical report showing that he sustained a number of lower back injuries. His condition is deteriorating, but he accepts the job as a retail store manager. This job requires lifting and standing for long periods.

Can the employer revoke the offer because the applicant would increase his risk of further back injury?

Analysis. Yes.

Few employers recognize this, but the likelihood of self-inflicted injury is a perfectly legal basis to reject someone. The employee's desires or threats should be ignored. Just be sure injury is likely, and that no minor alteration in the job duties or workplace can substantially reduce the risk.

Situation No. 7

The preemployment physical exam reveals a tumor on the applicant's lung that is probably malignant. He is an executive, and there is little immediate risk. However, the group health insurance premiums are extremely high due to the claims experience.

Can the applicant be rejected? Can he be required to pay his group insurance premiums?

Analysis. No to both questions.

Speculation about future risks or insurance claims are not a legal basis for rejecting an applicant. The tumor has nothing to do with the person's present ability to perform the job.

Requiring the employee to pay his group insurance premiums can only be done if all employees are charged. His future claim expense can't be offset by this payment.

Situation No. 8

The employer has a policy of keeping employees' medical records in their personnel files. A supervisor requests the records on someone he is considering for promotion to a field assignment. He wants to be sure the employee has no physical limitations.

Can he review the records?

Analysis. Probably.

This would be analogous to a preemployment physical. However, the medical records (even if from preemployment physical exams) can't be in the personnel files.

They must be (1) contained on separate forms, (2) in separate files, and (3) treated as confidential.

Medical information can be disclosed to medical, first aid, and safety personnel if an employee has a specific disability that might require emergency treatment.

Situation No. 9

A secretarial supervisor is complaining about the noise level in her work area. She is experiencing severe headaches for the first time in her life. The employer has received no other complaints, so he sends her to a doctor for a complete examination. The test reveals no medical reason for her headaches. However, her pain is affecting her ability to concentrate. The quality of her work is no longer acceptable.

The employer can move her to another area, but such a change will reduce her efficiency since she supervises others.

Can she be fired?

Analysis. Yes.

There is apparently no physical disability interfering with her work performance. Try to convince her of that, though. A complete diagnostic medical record is the best defense.

Situation No. 10

An applicant with one arm arrives at an interview for a position as a district manager. The interviewer asks whether having one arm affects the applicant's ability to drive. The applicant answered no. Then the interviewer asks for the applicant's driver's license number and the name of his automobile insurance carrier.

Are these interview inquiries permissible?

Analysis. Yes, no, and no.

Driving is a legitimate requirement of the job. If the interviewer asked *how* the disability affected the applicant's driving, he'd be out of line. But here he asked *whether* it affected his driving.

The interviewer can ask whether the applicant has a valid driver's license, but not the number. He can also ask whether the applicant can provide evidence of insurance after being hired, but not the carrier before a hiring.

Tricky, but that's why I wrote this book.

Situation No. 12

An applicant for the position of a bank loan officer had a partial paralysis on her right side (including her arm and hand) due to an inoperable nerve disorder. She was equally as qualified as another applicant, but her salary requirement was half as much. The employer favored hiring the other applicant because she had more promotion potential.

Must the employer hire the disabled applicant?

Analysis. Yes.

A loan officer has a desk job that can be performed fully with minor workplace alterations. A phone headset, left-handed desk, spring-loaded scissors, automatic page turner, revolving shelf, and a variety of other workstation changes would be required.

Lack of promotion potential as a hiring consideration here is synonymous with unequal employment opportunity.

Resources

ORGANIZATIONS

ABLEDATA
8455 Colesville Road
Silver Spring, MD 20910-3319
800/346-2742 or 800/227-0216
301/588-9284
*A consumer referral service that
maintains a data base of more
than 17,000 adaptive devices
from 2,000 companies.*

Accent on Information
P.O. Box 700
Bloomington, IL 61702
309/378-2961

ACTION
1100 Vermont Avenue, N.W.
Washington, DC 20525
800/424-8867

**Adaptive Device Locator
  System**
Academic Software
331 W. 2nd Street
Lexington, KY 40507
606/233-2332

**Administration on
  Developmental Disabilities**
Department of Health and
  Human Services
200 Independence Avenue, S.W.
Washington, DC 20201
202/245-2890
202/245-2897 (TDD)

**Advanced Rehabilitation
  Technology Network**
25825 Eshelman Avenue
Lomita, CA 90717
310/325-3058

Alliance for Technology Access
1128 Solano Avenue
Albany, CA 94706
510/528-0747

American Cancer Society
1599 Clifton Road, N.E.
Atlanta, GA 30329
800/227-2345

American Council of the Blind
1155 15th Street, N.W.
Washington, DC 20005
800/424-8666

**American Federation of Labor
& Congress of Industrial
Organizations**
815 16th Street, N.W.
Washington, DC 20006
202/637-5000

**American Foundation for
Technology Assistance**
Route 14, Box 230
Morganton, NC 28655
704/438-9697

**American Foundation for the
Blind**
15 W. 16th Street
New York, NY 10011
212/620-2000
212/620-2158 (TT)

**American Occupational Therapy
Association**
1383 Piccard Drive
Rockville, MD 20849
800/843-2682

American Paralysis Foundation
500 Morris
Springfield, NJ 07081
800/225-0292

**American Parkinson's Disease
Association**
60 Bay Street
Staten Island, NY 10301
800/223-2732

**American Physical Therapy
Association**
1111 N. Fairfax Street
Alexandria, VA 22314
703/684-2782

**American Printing House for
the Blind**
1839 Frankfort Avenue
Louisville, KY 40206
800/223-1839

**American Society of
Handicapped Physicians**
105 Morris Drive
Bastrop, LA 71220
318/281-4436

**American Speech-Language-
Hearing Association**
10801 Rockville Pike
Rockville, MD 20852
800/638-8255
301/897-5700

American Tinnitus Association
P.O. Box 5
Portland, OR 97207
503/248-9985

Apple Computer
Worldwide Disability Solutions
   Group
20525 Mariani Avenue
Cupertino, CA 95014
408/974-7910
408/974-7911 (TDD)

**Architectural and
   Transportation Barriers
   Compliance Board**
1331 F Street, N.W.
Washington, DC 20004
800/USA-ABLE
202/272-5434
*A federal entity; has a technical
assistance hotline for
organizations that must comply
with the ADA.*

Arthritis Foundation
1314 Spring Street, N.W.
Atlanta, GA 30309
800/283-7800

Assistive Device Center
6000 J Street
Sacramento, CA 95819
916/278-6422

**Assistive Technology
   Information Network**
University Hospital
The University of Iowa
Iowa City, IA 55242
800/331-3027

**Association for Education and
   Rehabilitation of the Blind
   and Visually Impaired**
206 N. Washington Street
Alexandria, VA 22314
703/548-1884

**Association for Mental
   Retardation**
500 E. Border
Arlington, TX 76010
817/261-6003

**Association for Retarded
   Citizens**
National Employment and
   Training Program
P.O. Box 6109
Arlington, TX 76005
817/640-0204
*A federally funded program
involved in training and placing
the disabled, with some 1,300
state and local chapters
nationwide.*

**Association of Persons in
   Supported Employment**
5001 W. Broad Street
Richmond, VA 23230
804/282-3655

**AT&T National Special Needs
   Center**
2001 Route 46
Parsippany, NJ 07054
800/233-1222 or 800/833-3232

Berkeley Planning Associates
440 Grand Avenue
Oakland, CA 94610
510/465-7884

Better Hearing Institute
P.O. Box 1840
Washington, DC 20013
800/327-9355

Braille Institute of America
741 N. Vermont Avenue
Los Angeles, CA 90029
213/663-1111

**Building Owners and Managers
  Association International**
1201 New York Avenue, N.W.
Washington, DC 20005
202/408-2662
Publications include ADA
Compliance Guidebook: A
Checklist for Your Building.

**Bureau of Services for Visually
  Impaired**
5535 Southwick Boulevard
Toledo, OH 43614
419/866-1669

Centers for Disease Control
Public Health Service
U.S. Department of Health and
  Human Services
1600 Clifton Road, N.E.
Atlanta, GA 30333
404/639-2237

**Clearinghouse on Computer
  Accommodations**
General Services Administration
18 and F Streets, N.W.
KGDO #2022
Washington, DC 20405
202/501-4906

**Clearinghouse on Disability
  Information**
U.S. Department of Education
Switzer Building
400 Maryland Avenue, S.W.
Washington, DC 20202
202/708-5366

Commission on Civil Rights
1121 Vermont Avenue, N.W.
Washington, DC 20425
202/376-8312

**Computer Electronic
  Accommodations Program**
Department of Defense
5109 Leesburg Pike
Falls Church, VA 22041
703/756-8811

**Congress of Organizations of
  the Physically Disabled**
16630 Beverly Drive
Tinley Park, IL 60477
708/532-3566

Council for Disability Rights
208 S. LaSalle Street
Chicago, IL 60604
312/444-9484

**Council of Better Business
  Bureaus**
4200 Wilson Boulevard
Arlington, VA 22203
703/276-0100

**Council of Citizens with Low
  Vision International**
1400 N. Drake Road
Kalamazoo, MI 49006
616/381-9566

**Council of State Administrators
  of Vocational Rehabilitation**
1055 Thomas Jefferson Street,
  N.W.
Washington, DC 20007
202/638-4634
*Call for information on state
vocational rehabilitation
agencies.*

Cystic Fibrosis Foundation
6931 Arlington Road
Bethesda, MD 20814
800/344-4823

Deafness and Communicative Disorders Branch
U.S. Department of Education
Rehabilitation Services
330 C Street, S.W.
Washington, DC 20202
202/732-1401
202/732-1330 (TDD)

Direct Link for the Disabled
P.O. Box 1036
Solvang, CA 93464
805/688-1603

Disabilities Rights Education and Defense Fund
2212 6th Street
Berkeley, CA 94710
800/466-4232
Offers free material and advice.

Dole Foundation for Employment of People with Disabilities
1819 H Street, N.W.
Washington, DC 20006
202/457-0318

Electronic Industries Foundation
919 18th Street
Washington, DC 20006
202/955-5816

Employment Law Center
1663 Mission Street
San Francisco, CA 94103
415/864-8848

Equal Employment Opportunity Commission
1801 L Street, N.W.
Washington, DC 20507
ADA Helpline: 1-800/669-EEOC
800/800-3302 (TDD)
202/663-4900
202/663-4264 (publications)
*For $25 the EEOC offers a technical assistance manual and a large resource directory.
Booklets available include* The ADA: Your Responsibilities as an Employer; The ADA: Questions and Answers; *and,* The ADA: Your Rights as an Individual with a Disability.

Federal Communications Commission
Office of Public Affairs
1919 M Street, N.W.
Washington, DC 20036
202/532-7260 or 202/632-6999

Federation of the Handicapped
211 W. 14th Street
New York, NY 10011
212/727-4200
212/727-4324 (TDD)

Foundation on Employment and Disability
3820 Del Amo Boulevard
Torrance, CA 90503
310/214-3430

Goodwill Industries of America
9200 Wisconsin Avenue
Bethesda, MD 20814-3896
301/530-6500
301/530-0836 (TDD)

Handicapped Assistance Loan Program
Small Business Administration
409 3rd Street, S.W.
Washington, DC 20416
202/205-6570

HEALTH Resource Center
(Higher Education and the Handicapped)
Project of the American Council on Education
Department of Education
1 Dupont Circle, N.W.
Washington, DC 20036
800/544-3284

Huntington's Disease Society of America
140 W. 22nd Street
New York, NY 10011
800/345-4372

IAM Cares (International Association of Machinists and Aerospace Workers Handicapped Youth)
1300 Connecticut Avenue, N.W.
Washington, DC 20036
202/857-5200

IBM National Support Center for Persons with Disabilities
P.O. Box 2150
Atlanta, GA 30055
800/426-2133
IBM-funded nonprofit agency provides free information on thousands of computer hardware and software accommodation devices, most of which are not IBM products.

Independent Visually Impaired Enterprises
1155 15th Street, N.W.
Washington, DC 20005
202/467-5081

Internal Revenue Service U.S. Department of the Treasury
1111 Constitution Avenue, N.W.
Washington, DC 20224
202/566-3292
800/829-4059 (TDD)

International Association of Business, Industry and Rehabilitation
P.O. Box 15242
Washington, DC 20003
202/543-6353

International Association of Jewish Vocational Services
101 Gary Court
Staten Island, NY 10314
718/370-0437

International Association of Laryngectomies
1599 Clifton Road, N.E.
Atlanta, GA 30329
404/320-3333

International Center for the Disabled
340 E. 24th Street
New York, NY 10010
212/679-0100

International Polio Network
5100 Oakland Avenue
St. Louis, MO 63110
314/361-0475

Institute for Rehabilitation and Disability Management
229½ Pennsylvania Avenue, S.E.
Washington, DC 20003
202/408-9320
Publishes The Disability Management Sourcebook.

Job Accommodation Network
P.O. Box 6123
809 Allen Hall
West Virginia University
Morgantown, WV 26506-6123
800/526-7234
A service of the President's Committee on Employment of People with Disabilities. The Job Accommodation Network (JAN) provides free consulting services to employers seeking to accommodate workers with disabilities. JAN also maintains a large computer data base of companies across the country that have accommodated workers.

Job Training Partnership Act Programs
Office of Job Training Programs
Employment and Training Administration
U.S. Department of Labor
200 Constitution Avenue, N.W.
Washington, DC 20210
202/535-0580

Joseph P. Kennedy, Jr., Foundation
1350 New York Avenue, N.W.
Washington, DC 20005
202/393-1250

Just One Break
373 Park Avenue South
New York, NY 10016
212/725-2500

Leukemia Society of America
733 3rd Avenue
New York, NY 10017
800/955-4572

Lupus Foundation of America
4 Research Place
Rockville, MD 20850
800/558-0121

Mainstream, Inc.
3 Bethesda Metro Center
Bethesda, MD 20814
301/654-2400
A private, nonprofit organization that helps disabled individuals move into the workplace; publishes guides for employers on hiring the disabled.

Mental Health & Retardation Services
State Office Building, 5th Floor
Topeka, KS 66612
913/296-3774

Mental Health Policy Resource Center
1730 Rhode Island Avenue, N.W.
Washington, DC 20036
202/775-8826

Mental Retardation Associations of America
211 E. 300 South
Salt Lake City, UT 84111
801/328-1575

Muscular Dystrophy Association
3561 E. Sunrise Drive
Tucson, AZ 85718
800/223-6666

**National Alliance for the
  Mentally Ill**
2101 Wilson Boulevard
Arlington, VA 22201
703/524-7600

**National Amputation
  Foundation**
1245 150th Street
Whitestone, NY 11357
718/767-0596

**National Association for
  Visually Handicapped**
22 W. 21st Street
New York, NY 10010
212/889-3141

**National Association of
  Rehabilitation Facilities**
P.O. Box 17675
Washington, DC 20041
703/648-9300

**National Association of the
  Deaf**
814 Thayer Avenue
Silver Spring, MD 20910
301/587-1788

**National Association of the
  Physically Handicapped**
Bethesda Scarlet Oaks
440 Lafayette Avenue
Cincinnati, OH 45220
513/961-8040

National Braille Association
1290 University Avenue
Rochester, NY 14607
716/473-0900

National Braille Press
88 Saint Stephen Street
Boston, MA 02115
617/266-6160

**National Cancer Care
  Foundation**
1180 Avenue of the Americas
New York, NY 10036
212/221-3300

**National Center for Disability
  Services**
201 I. U. Willetts Road
Albertson, NY 11507
516/747-5355
516/746-3298 (TT)

**National Center for Law and the
  Deaf**
800 Florida Avenue, N.E.
Washington, DC 20002
202/651-5373

**National Center for Learning
  Disabilities**
99 Park Avenue
New York, NY 10016
212/687-7211

National Center for State Courts
ADA Clearinghouse and
  Resource Center
300 Newport Avenue
Williamsburg, VA 23185
804/253-2000

National Center on Employment of the Deaf
Rochester Institute of
 Technology
Department of Education
P.O. Box 9887
Rochester, NY 14623
716/475-6205
716/475-6500 (TDD)

National Council on Disability
800 Independence Avenue, S.W.
Washington, DC 20591
202/267-3846

National Council on Independent Living
Troy Atrium
4th Street and Broadway
Troy, NY 12180
518/274-1979
518/274-0701 (TT)

National Depressive and Manic Depressive Association
730 N. Franklin Street
Chicago, IL 60610
312/642-0049

National Down Syndrome Congress
1800 Dempster Street
Park Ridge, IL 60068
800/232-6372

National Down Syndrome Society
666 Broadway
New York, NY 10012
800/221-4602

National Easter Seal Society
70 E. Lake Street
Chicago, IL 60601
312/726-6200
312/726-4258 (TDD)

National Federation of the Blind
Job Opportunities for the Blind
1800 Johnson Street
Baltimore, MD 21230
800/638-7518
410/659-9314

National Health Council
1730 M Street, N.W.
Washington, DC 20036
202/785-3910

National Industries for the Blind
524 Hamburg Turnpike
Wayne, NJ 07474
201/595-9200

National Industries for the Severely Handicapped
2235 Cedar Lane
Vienna, VA 22182
703/560-6800

National Information Center on Deafness
Gallaudet University
800 Florida Avenue, N.E.
Washington, DC 20002
202/651-5051
202/651-5052 (TDD)

National Information System
Center for Developmental
 Disabilities
University of South Carolina
Benson Building, 1st Floor
Columbia, SC 29208
803/777-4435

National Institute for the Deaf
Rochester Institute of
   Technology
One Lamb Memorial Drive
P.O. Box 9887
Rochester, NY 14623
716/475-6824

**National Institute on Disability
   and Rehabilitation Research**
400 Maryland Avenue, S.W.
Washington, DC 20202-2572
202/732-5801
202/732-5316 (TDD)
*Operates 10 regional technical
assistance centers (see below).
Your toll-free call to 1-800/949-
4232 will ring through to the
facility serving your area.*

National Kidney Foundation
30 E. 33rd Street
New York, NY 10016
800/622-9010

**National Leadership Coalition
   on AIDS**
1730 M Street, N.W.
Washington, DC 20036
202/429-0930

**National Library Services for
   the Blind and Physically
   Handicapped**
The Library of Congress
1291 Taylor Street, N.W.
Washington, DC 20542
202/707-5100
202/707-0744 (TDD)

**National Mental Health
   Association**
1021 Prince Street
Alexandria, VA 22314
703/684-7722

**National Multiple Sclerosis
   Society**
205 E. 42nd Street
New York, NY 10017
800/624-8326

**National Network of Learning
   Disabled Adults**
808 N. 82nd Street
Scottsdale, AZ 85257
602/941-5112

**National Organization on
   Disability**
910 16th Street, N.W.
Washington, DC 20006
202/293-5960
202/293-5968 (TDD)
*Operates an information
clearinghouse.*

National Parkinson Foundation
1501 NW 9th Avenue
Miami, FL 33136
800/327-4545

**National Rehabilitation
   Association**
633 State Washington Street
Alexandria, VA 22314
703/836-0750
703/836-0852 (TDD)

**National Rehabilitation
   Information Center**
8455 Colesville Road
Silver Spring, MD 20910-3319
301/588-9284

National Scoliosis Foundation
72 Mt. Auburn Street
Watertown, MA 02172
617/926-0397

National Spinal Cord Injury Association
600 W. Cummings Park
Woburn, MA 01801
800/962-9629

National Stroke Association
300 E. Hampden Avenue
Englewood, CO 80110
800/367-1990

National Stuttering Project
4601 Irving Street
San Francisco, CA 94122
415/566-5324

National Technical Information Service
U.S. Department of Commerce
5285 Port Royal Road
Springfield, VA 22161
703/487-4650
Publications include Guide for Administering Employment Examinations to Handicapped Individuals, *and* Testing the Handicapped for Employment Purposes: Adaptations for Persons with Motor Handicaps.

National Tuberous Sclerosis Association
8000 Corporate Drive
Landover, MD 20785
800/225-6872

Office of Federal Contract Compliance Programs Department of Labor
200 Constitution Avenue, N.W.
Washington, DC 20210
202/523-9501

Orton Dyslexia Society
8600 LaSalle Road
Baltimore, MD 21204
800/222-3123

Parkinson's Disease Foundation
640 W. 168th Street
New York, NY 10032
800/457-6676

People First International
P.O. Box 12642
Salem, OR 97309
503/588-5288

Polio Society
4200 Wisconsin Avenue, N.W.
P.O. Box 106273
Washington, DC 20016
301/897-8180

President's Committee on Employment of People with Disabilities
1331 F Street, N.W.
Washington, DC 20004-1107
202/376-6200
202/376-6205 (TDD)
Provides information, referral, and technical assistance to employers and employees with disabilities. Extensive list of free publications.

President's Committee on Mental Retardation
330 Independence Avenue, S.W.
Washington, DC 20201-0001
202/619-0634

Professional Rehabilitation Sector
P.O. Box 697
Brookline, MA 02146
617/566-4432

Project Access
303 E. Wacker Drive
Chicago, IL 60601
312/565-0815
Maintains the Computer Information Center, a comprehensive data base of ADA information from a variety of sources. An annual fee of $100 allows unlimited access to the data base.

Recording for the Blind
20 Roszel Road
Princeton, NJ 08540
609/452-0606

Rehabilitation Services Administration
U.S. Department of Education
Switzer Building
330 C Street, S.W.
Washington, DC 20202
202/732-1282

Research and Training Center for Accessible Housing
P.O. Box 8613
North Carolina University
Raleigh, NC 27695-8613
919/515-3082

Self-Help for Hard of Hearing People
7800 Wisconsin Avenue
Bethesda, MD 20814
301/657-2248

Senate Subcommittee on Disability Policy
113 Hart Senate Office Building
Washington, DC 20510
202/224-6265
202/224-3457 (TDD)

Sensory Aids Foundation
399 Sherman Avenue
Palo Alto, CA 94306
415/329-0430

Short Stature Foundation
17200 Jamboree Road #J
Irvine, CA 92714
800/243-9273

Sjogren's Syndrome Foundation
382 Main Street
Port Washington, NY 11050
516/767-2866

Small Business Administration
409 3rd Street, S.W.
Washington, DC 20416
202/205-6530

Small Business Legislative Council
1156 15th Street, N.W.
Washington, DC 20005
202/639-8500

Society for the Advancement of Travel for the Handicapped
347 5th Avenue
New York, NY 10016
212/447-7284

Spina Bifida Association of America
1700 Rockville Pike
Rockville, MD 20852
800/621-3141

Stroke Clubs International
805 12th Street
Galveston, TX 77550
409/762-1022

Telecommunications for the Deaf
8719 Colesville Road
Silver Spring, MD 20910
301/589-3786

Tourette Syndrome Association
42-40 Bell Boulevard
Bayside, NY 11361
800/237-0717

Travel Industry and Disabled Exchange
5435 Donna Avenue
Tarzanna, CA 91356
818/343-6339

United Cerebral Palsy Association
1522 K Street, N.W.
Washington, DC 20005
800/872-5827

U.S. Chamber of Commerce
1615 H Street, N.W.
Washington, DC 20062-2000
800/638-6582
Publications include What Business Must Know about the ADA.

U.S. Department of Justice
Civil Rights Division
ADA Information Line
P.O. Box 66118
Washington, DC 20039
202/514-0301
To get a copy of the Americans with Disabilities Act, contact the Coordination & Review Section.

U.S. Department of Transportation
400 7th Street, S.W.
Washington, DC 20590
202/366-9305

Veterans Employment and Training Service U.S. Department of Labor
500 C Street, N.W.
Washington, DC 20001
202/727-3342

Wage and Hour Division
Employment
Standards Administration
U.S. Department of Labor
200 Constitution Avenue, N.W.
Washington, DC 20210
202/523-8727
Administers regulation governing the employment of people with disabilities in sheltered workshops and the disabled workers industries.

Western Law Center for the Handicapped
1441 W. Olympic Boulevard
Los Angeles, CA 90015
213/736-1031

World Institute on Disability
510 16th Street
Oakland, CA 94612
415/763-4100

World Rehabilitation Fund
386 Park Avenue South
New York, NY 10016
212/679-2934

NATIONAL INSTITUTE ON DISABILITY AND REHABILITATION RESEARCH REGIONAL DISABILITY AND BUSINESS TECHNICAL ASSISTANCE CENTERS

Region 1: New England
(CT, ME, MA, NH, RI, VT)
University of South Maine
Institute of Public Affairs
145 Newbury Street
Portland, ME 04101
207/874-6535

Region 2: Northeast
(NJ, NY, PR, VI)
United Cerebral Palsy
  Association
354 S. Broad Street
Trenton, NJ 08608
609/392-4004
609/392-7044 (TDD)

Region 3: Mid-Atlantic
(DE, DC, MD, PA, VA, WV)
Independence Center of
  Northern Virginia
2111 Wilson Boulevard
Arlington, VA 22201
703/525-3268

Region 4: Southeast
(AL, FL, GA, KY, MS, NC, SC, TN)
United Cerebral Palsy
  Association
1776 Peachtree Street
Atlanta, GA 30309
404/888-0022
404/888-9007 (TDD)

Region 5: Great Lakes
(IL, IN, MI, MN, OH, WI)
University of Illinois at Chicago
1640 W. Roosevelt Road
Chicago, IL 60608
312/413-1407
312/413-0453 (TDD)

Region 6: Southwest
(AR, LA, NM, OK, TX)
Institute for Rehabilitation and
  Research
2323 S. Shepherd Boulevard
Houston, TX 77019
713/520-0232
713/520-5136 (TDD)

Region 7: Great Plains
(IA, KS, NE, MO)
University of Missouri at
  Columbia
4816 Santana Drive
Columbia, MO 65203
314/882-3600

Region 8: Rocky Mountain
(CO, MT, ND, SD, UT, WY)
Meeting the Challenge, Inc.
3630 Sinton Road
Colorado Springs, CO 80907
719/444-0252

Region 9: Pacific
(AZ, CA, HI, NV, Pacific Basin)
Berkeley Planning Associates
440 Grand Avenue
Oakland, CA 94610
510/465-7884
800/949-4232 (TDD)

Region 10: Northwest
(AK, ID, OR, WA)
Governor's Committee on
    Disability Issues and
    Employment
P.O. Box 9046
Olympia, WA 98507
206/438-3168
206/438-3167 (TDD)
800/HELP-ADA

PUBLICATIONS

Allen, Jeffrey G., ed. *The Employee Termination Handbook.* New York: John Wiley & Sons, 1986.

Bakaly, Charles G., Jr. *The Modern Law of Employment Relationships.* Englewood Cliffs, NJ: Prentice-Hall, 1989, with 1991 supplement. ($85.)

Fasman, Zachary. *What Business Must Know About the ADA: 1992 Compliance Guide.* Washington, DC: U.S. Chamber of Commerce, 1992. ($33.) To order, call 908/638-6582.

Frierson, James G. *Employer's Guide to the Americans with Disabilities Act.* Washington, DC: Bureau of National Affairs, 1992. ($45.)

Hogan, Patricia, ed. *Implementing the Employment Provisions of the American with Disabilities Act.* New York: Faulkner & Gray, 1991. ($87.) To order, call 800/535-8403.

Johnson, Mary, ed. *People with Disabilities Explain It for You.* Louisville, Ky.: Avocado Press, 1992. ($15.95.) To order, call 800/338-5412.

Job Analysis under the Americans with Disabilities Act. Rosemont, Ill.: London House, 1991. (Free.) To order, call 800/221-8378.

Krementz, Jill. *How It Feels to Live with a Physical Disability.* New York: Simon & Schuster, 1992. ($18.) To order, call 800/338-5412.

Lawson, Joseph W.R. *The Manager's Guide to the Americans with Disabilities Act.* Chicago: Dartnell, 1991. ($129.)

LOMA (previously Life Office Management Association). *The Human Resources Manager's Guide to ADA Compliance.* Atlanta: LOMA, 1992. ($90.)

————. *A Manager's Guide to the ADA: A Practical Approach.* Atlanta: LOMA, 1992. ($10.)

————. *ADA: The Simple Facts.* Atlanta: LOMA, 1992. ($3.) To order LOMA publications, call 404/984-3780.

Lotito, Michael, et al. *Making the ADA Work for You*, 2d ed: Northridge, Calif.: Milt Wright & Associates, 1992. ($39.50.)

Meeting the Needs of Employees with Disabilities. Lexington, Mass.: Resources for Rehabilitation, 1991. ($42.95.) To order, call 617/862-6455.

Morrisey, Patricia. *Human Resource Executive's Survival Guide to the Americans with Disabilities Act.* Horsham, Pa.: LRP Publications, 1992. ($135.)

Perritt, Henry H., Jr. *Americans with Disabilities Act Handbook*, 2d ed. New York: John Wiley & Sons, 1991.

Personnel Selection under the Americans with Disabilities Act. Rosemont, Ill.: London House, 1992. (Free.) To order, call 800/221-8378.

Pimentel, Richard, et al. *What Managers and Supervisors Need to Know about the ADA.* Northridge, Calif.: Milt Wright & Associates, 1992. ($18.50.)

The New Supervisor's EEO Handbook. New York: Executive Enterprises, 1992. ($9.95.) To order, call 800/332-1105.

Telecommunications Devices for the Deaf: A Guide to Selection, Ordering and Installation. Washington, DC: U.S. Architectural and Transportation Barriers Compliance Board. To order, call 202/272-5434.

Titles I and III of the Americans with Disabilities Act

(P.L. 101–336, approved July 26, 1990)

Preface and Part I. Employment

Chapter 126 [of 42 U.S. Code]. Americans with Disabilities

§ 12101. Short title; Table of contents

[Sec. 1] (a) This act may be cited as the "Americans with Disabilities Act of 1990."

(b) Table of Contents [Omitted.]

§ 12102. Findings and purposes

[Sec. 2] (a) The Congress finds that—

(1) some 43,000,000 Americans have one or more physical or mental disabilities, and this number is increasing as the population as a whole is growing older;

(2) historically, society has tended to isolate and segregate individuals with disabilities, and, despite some improvements, such forms of discrimination against individuals with disabilities continue to be a serious and pervasive social problem;

(3) discrimination against individuals with disabilities persists in

such critical areas as employment, housing, public accommodations, education, transportation, communication, recreation, institutionalization, health services, voting, and access to public services;

(4) unlike individuals who have experienced discrimination on the basis of race, color, sex, national origin, religion, or age, individuals who have experienced discrimination on the basis of disability have often had no legal recourse to redress such discrimination;

(5) individuals with disabilities continually encounter various forms of discrimination, including outright intentional exclusion, the discriminatory effects of architectural, transportation, and communication barriers, overprotective rules and policies, failure to make modifications to existing facilities and practices, exclusionary qualification standards and criteria, segregation, and regulation to lesser services, programs, activities, benefits, jobs, or other opportunities;

(6) census data, national polls, and other studies have documented that people with disabilities, as a group, occupy an inferior status in our society, vocationally, economically, and educationally;

(7) individuals with disabilities are a discrete and insular minority who have been faced with restrictions and limitations, subjected to a history of purposeful unequal treatment, and regulated to a position of political powerlessness in our society, based on characteristics that are beyond the control of such individuals and resulting from stereotypic assumptions not truly indicative of the individual ability of such individuals to participate in, and contribute to, society;

(8) the Nation's proper goals regarding individuals with disabilities are to assure equality of opportunity, full participation, independent living, and economic self-sufficiency for such individuals; and

(9) the continuing existence of unfair and unnecessary discrimination and prejudice denies people with disabilities the opportunity to compete on an equal basis and to pursue those opportunities for which our free society is justifiably famous, and costs the United States billions of dollars in unnecessary expenses, resulting from dependency and non-productivity.

(b) It is the purpose of this Act—

(1) to provide a clear and comprehensive national mandate for the elimination of discrimination against individuals with disabilities;

(2) to provide clear, strong, consistent, enforceable standards addressing discrimination against individuals with disabilities;

(3) to ensure that the Federal Government plays a central role in enforcing the standards established in this Act on behalf of individuals with disabilities; and

(4) to invoke the sweep of congressional authority, including the power to enforce the fourteenth amendment and to regulate commerce, in order to address the major areas of discrimination faced day-to-day by people with disabilities.

§ 12103. Definitions

[Sec. 3] As used in this Act:

(1) The term "auxiliary aids and services" includes—

(A) qualified interpreters or other effective methods of making aurally delivered materials available to individuals with hearing impairments;

(B) qualified readers, taped texts, or other effective methods of making visually delivered materials available to individuals with visual impairments;

(C) acquisition or modification of equipment or devices; and

(D) other similar services and actions.

(2) The term "disability" means, with respect to an individual—

(A) a physical or mental impairment that substantially limits one or more of the major life activities of such individual;

(B) a record of such an impairment; or

(C) being regarded as having such an impairment.

(3) The term "State" means each of the several States, the District of Columbia, the Commonwealth of Puerto Rico, Guam, American Samoa, the Virgin Islands, the Trust Territory of the Pacific Islands, and the Commonwealth of the Northern Mariana Islands.

Title I. Employment

§ 12111. Definitions

[Sec. 101] As used in this title:

(1) The term "Commission" means the Equal Employment Opportunity Commission established by section 705 of the Civil Rights Act of 1964 (42 U.S.C. 2000e-4).

(2) The term "covered entity" means an employer, employment agency, labor organization, or joint labor-management committee.

(3) The term "direct threat" means a significant risk to the health or safety of others that cannot be eliminated by reasonable accommodation.

(4) The term "employee" means an individual employed by an employer.

(5)(A) The term "employer" means a person engaged in an industry affecting commerce who has 15 or more employees for each working day in each of 20 or more calendar weeks in the current or preceding calendar year, and any agent of such person, except that, for two years following the effective date of this title, an employer means a person engaged in an industry affecting commerce who has 25 or more employees for each working day in each of 20 or more calendar weeks in the current or preceding year, and any agent of such person.

(B) The term "employer" does not include—

(i) the United States, a corporation wholly owned by the government of the United States, or an Indian tribe; or

(ii) a bona fide private membership club (other than a labor organization) that is exempt from taxation under section 501(c) of the Internal Revenue Code of 1986.

(6)(A) The term "illegal use of drugs" means the use of drugs, the possession or distribution of which is unlawful under the Controlled Substances Act (21 U.S.C. 812). Such term does not include the use of a drug taken under supervision by a licensed health care professional, or other uses authorized by the Controlled Substances Act or other provisions of Federal law.

(B) The term "drug" means a controlled substance, as defined in schedule I through V of section 202 of the Controlled Substances Act.

(7) The terms "person," "labor organization," "employment agency," "commerce," and "industry affecting commerce," shall have the same meaning given such terms in section 701 of the Civil Rights Act of 1964 (42 U.S.C. 2000e).

(8) The term "qualified individual with a disability" means an individual with a disability who, with or without reasonable accommodation, can perform the essential functions of the employment position that such individual holds or desires. For the purposes of this title, consideration shall be given to the employer's judgment as to what functions of a job are essential, and if an employer has prepared a written description before advertising or interviewing applicants for the job, this description shall be considered evidence of the essential functions of the job.

(9) The term "reasonable accommodation" may include—

(A) making existing facilities used by employees readily accessible to and usable by individuals with disabilities; and

(B) job restructuring, part-time or modified work schedules, reassignment to a vacant position, acquisition or modification of equipment or devices, appropriate adjustment or modifications of examinations, training materials or policies, the provision of qualified readers or interpreters, and other similar accommodations for individuals with disabilities.

(10)(A) The term "undue hardship" means an action requiring significant difficulty or expense, when considered in light of the factors set forth in subparagraph (B).

(B) In determining whether an accommodation would impose an undue hardship on a covered entity, factors to be considered include—

> (i) the nature and cost of the accommodation needed under this Act;

> (ii) the overall financial resources of the facility or facilities involved in the provision of the reasonable accommodation; the number of persons employed at such facility; the effect on expenses and resources, or the impact otherwise of such accommodation upon the operation of the facility;

> (iii) the overall financial resources of the covered entity; the overall size of the business of a covered entity with respect to the number of its employees; the number, type, and location of its facilities; and

> (iv) the type of operation or operations of the covered entity, including the composition, structure, and functions of the workforce of such entity; the geographic separateness, administrative, or fiscal relationship of the facility or facilities in question to the covered entity.

§ 12112. Discrimination

[Sec. 102] (a) No covered entity shall discriminate against a qualified individual with a disability because of the disability of such individual in regard to job application procedures, the hiring, advancement, or discharge of employees, employee compensation, job training, and other terms, conditions, and privileges of employment.

(b) As used in subsection (a), the term "discriminate" includes—

(1) limiting, segregating, or classifying a job applicant or employee in a way that adversely affects the opportunities or status of such applicant or employee because of the disability of such applicant or employee;

(2) participating in a contractual or other arrangement or relationship that has the effect of subjecting a covered entity's qualified applicant or employee with a disability to the discrimination prohibited by this title (such relationship includes a relationship with an employment or referral agency, labor union, an organization providing fringe benefits

to an employee of the covered entity, or an organization providing training and apprenticeship programs);

(3) utilizing standards, criteria, or methods of administration—

(A) that have the effect of discrimination on the basis of disability; or

(B) that perpetuate the discrimination of others who are subject to common administrative control;

(4) excluding or otherwise denying equal jobs or benefits to a qualified individual because of the known disability of an individual with whom the qualified individual is known to have a relationship or association;

(5)(A) not making reasonable accommodations to the known physical or mental limitations of an otherwise qualified individual with a disability who is an applicant or employee, unless such covered entity can demonstrate that the accommodation would impose an undue hardship on the operation of the business of such covered entity; or

(B) denying employment opportunities to a job applicant or employee who is an otherwise qualified individual with a disability, if such denial is based on the need of such covered entity to make reasonable accommodation to the physical or mental impairments of the employee or applicant;

(6) using qualification standards, employment tests or other selection criteria that screen out or tend to screen out an individual with a disability or a class of individuals with disabilities unless the standard, test or other selection criteria, as used by the covered entity, is shown to be job-related for the position in question and is consistent with business necessity; and

(7) failing to select and administer tests concerning employment in the most effective manner to ensure that, when such test is administered to a job applicant or employee who has a disability that impairs sensory, manual, or speaking skills, such test results accurately reflect the skills, aptitude, or whatever other factor of such applicant or employee that such test purports to measure, rather than reflecting the impaired sensory, manual, or speaking skills of such employee or applicant (except where such skills are the factors that the test purports to measure).

(c)(1) The prohibition against discrimination as referred to in subsection (a) shall include medical examinations and inquiries.

(2)(A) Except as provided in paragraph (3), a covered entity shall not conduct a medical examination or make inquiries of a job applicant as to whether such applicant is an individual with a disability or as to the nature or severity of such disability.

(B) A covered entity may make preemployment inquiries into the ability of an applicant to perform job-related functions.

(3) A covered entity may require a medical examination after an offer of employment has been made to a job applicant and prior to the commencement of the employment duties of such applicant, and may condition an offer of employment on the results of such examination, if—

(A) all entering employees are subjected to such an examination regardless of disability;

(B) information obtained regarding the medical condition or history of the applicant is collected and maintained on separate forms and in separate medical files and is treated as a confidential medical record, except that—

(i) supervisors and managers may be informed regarding necessary restrictions on the work or duties of employee and necessary accommodations;

(ii) first aid and safety personnel may be informed, when appropriate, if the disability might require emergency treatment; and

(iii) government officials investigating compliance with this Act shall be provided relevant information on request; and

(C) the results of such examination are used only in accordance with this title.

(4)(A) A covered entity shall not require a medical examination and shall not make inquiries of an employee as to whether such employee is an individual with a disability or as to the nature or severity of the disability, unless such examination or inquiry is shown to be job-related and consistent with business necessity.

(B) A covered entity may conduct voluntary medical examinations, including voluntary medical histories, which are part of an employee health program available to employees at that work site. A covered entity may make inquiries into the ability of an employee to perform job-related functions.

(C) Information obtained under subparagraph (B) regarding the medical condition or history of any employee are subject to the requirements of subparagraphs (B) and (C) of paragraph (3).

§ 12113. Defenses

[Sec. 103] (a) It may be a defense to a charge of discrimination under this Act that an alleged application of qualification standards, tests, or selection criteria that screen out or tend to screen out or otherwise deny a job or benefit to an individual with a disability has been shown to be job-related and consistent with business necessity, and such performance cannot be accomplished by reasonable accommodation, as required under this title.

(b) The term "qualification standards" may include a requirement that an individual shall not pose a direct threat to the health or safety of other individuals in the workplace.

(c)(1) This title shall not prohibit a religious corporation, association, educational institution, or society from giving preference in employment to individuals of a particular religion to perform work connected with the carrying on by such corporation, association, educational institution, or society of its activities.

(2) Under this title, a religious organization may require that all applicants and employees conform to the religious tenets of such organization.

(d)(1) The Secretary of Health and Human Services, not later than 6 months after the date of enactment of this Act, shall—

(A) review all infectious and communicable diseases which may be transmitted through handling the food supply;

(B) publish a list of infectious and communicable diseases which are transmitted through handling the food supply;

(C) publish the methods by which such diseases are transmitted; and

(D) widely disseminate such information regarding the list of diseases and their modes of transmissability to the general public.

Such list shall be updated annually.

(2) In any case in which an individual has an infectious or communicable disease that is transmitted to others through the handling of food, that is included on the list developed by the Secretary of Health and Human Services under paragraph (1), and which cannot be eliminated by reasonable accommodation, a covered entity may refuse to assign or continue to assign such individual to a job involving food handling.

(3) Nothing in this Act shall be construed to preempt, modify, or amend any State, county, or local law, ordinance, or regulation applicable to food handling which is designed to protect the public health from individuals who pose a significant risk to the health or safety of others, which cannot be eliminated by reasonable accommodation, pursuant to the list of infectious or communicable diseases and the modes of transmissability published by the Secretary of Health and Human Services.

§ 12114. Illegal use of drugs and alcohol

[**Sec. 104**] (a) For purposes of this title, the term "qualified individual with disability" shall not include any employee or applicant who is currently engaging in the illegal use of drugs, when the covered entity acts on the basis of such use.

(b) Nothing in subsection (a) shall be construed to exclude as a qualified individual with a disability an individual who—

(1) has successfully completed a supervised drug rehabilitation program and is no longer engaging in the illegal use of drugs, or has otherwise been rehabilitated successfully and is no longer engaging in such use;

(2) is participating in a supervised rehabilitation program and is no longer engaging in such use; or

(3) is erroneously regarded as engaging in such use, but is not engaging in such use;

except that it shall not be a violation of this Act for a covered entity to adopt or administer reasonable policies or procedures, including but not limited to drug testing, designed to ensure that an individual described in paragraph (1) or (2) is no longer engaging in the illegal use of drugs.

(c) A covered entity—

(1) may prohibit the illegal use of drugs and the use of alcohol at the workplace by all employees;

(2) may require that employees shall not be under the influence of alcohol or be engaging in the illegal use of drugs at the workplace;

(3) may require that employees behave in conformance with the requirements established under the Drug-Free Workplace Act of 1988 (41 U.S.C. 701 et seq.);

(4) may hold an employee who engages in the illegal use of drugs or who is an alcoholic to the same qualification standards for employment or job performance and behavior that such entity holds other employees, even if any unsatisfactory performance or behavior is related to the drug use or alcoholism of such employee; and

(5) may, with respect to Federal regulations regarding alcohol and the illegal use of drugs, require that—

(A) employees comply with the standards established in such regulations of the Department of Defense, if the employees of the covered entity are employed in an industry subject to such regulations, including complying with regulations (if any) that apply to employment in sensitive positions in such an industry, in the case of employees of the covered entity who are employed in such positions (as defined in the regulations of the Department of Defense);

(B) employees comply with the standards established in such regulations of the Nuclear Regulatory Commission, if the employees of the covered entity are employed in an industry subject to such regulations, including complying with regulations (if any) that apply to employment in sensitive positions in such an industry, in the case of employees of the covered entity who are employed in such positions (as defined in the regulations of the Nuclear Regulatory Commission); and

(C) employees comply with the standards established in such regulations of the Department of Transportation, if the employees of the covered entity are employed in a transportation industry subject to such regulations, including complying with such regulations (if any) that apply to employment in sensitive positions in such an industry, in the case of employees of the covered entity who are employed in such positions (as defined in the regulations of the Department of Transportation).

(d)(1) For purposes of this title, a test to determine the illegal use of drugs shall not be considered a medical examination.

(2) Nothing in this title shall be construed to encourage, prohibit, or authorize the conducting of drug testing for the illegal use of drugs by job applicants or employees or making employment decisions based on such test results.

(e) Nothing in this title shall be construed to encourage, prohibit, restrict, or authorize the otherwise lawful exercise by entities subject to the jurisdiction of the Department of Transportation of authority to—

(1) test employees of such entities in, and applicants for, positions involving safety-sensitive duties for the illegal use of drugs and for on-duty impairment by alcohol; and

(2) remove such persons who test positive for illegal use of drugs and on-duty impairment by alcohol pursuant to paragraph (1) from safety-sensitive duties in implementing subsection (c).

§ 12115. Posting notices

[Sec. 105] Every employer, employment agency, labor organization, or joint labor-management committee covered under this title shall post notices in an accessible format to applicants, employees, and members describing the applicable provisions of this Act, in the manner prescribed by section 711 of the Civil Rights Act of 1964 (42 U.S.C. 2000e-10).

§ 12116. Regulations

[**Sec. 106**] Not later than 1 year after the date of enactment of this Act, the Commission shall issue regulations in an accessible format to carry out this title in accordance with subchapter II of chapter 5 of title 5, United States Code.

§ 12117. Enforcement

[**Sec. 107**] (a) The powers, remedies, and procedures set forth in sections 705, 706, 707, 709, and 710 of the Civil Rights Act of 1964 (42 U.S.C. 2000e-4, 2000e-5, 2000e-6, 2000e-8, and 2000e-9) shall be the powers, remedies, and procedures this title provides to the Commission, to the Attorney General, or to any person alleging discrimination on the basis of disability in violation of any provision of this Act, or regulations promulgated under section 106, concerning employment.

(b) The agencies with enforcement authority for actions which allege employment discrimination under this title and under the Rehabilitation Act of 1973 shall develop procedures to ensure that administrative complaints filed under this title and under the Rehabilitation Act of 1973 are dealt with in a manner that avoids duplication of effort and prevents imposition of inconsistent or conflicting standards for the same requirements under this title and the Rehabilitation Act of 1973. The Commission, the Attorney General, and the Office of Federal Contract Compliance Programs shall establish such coordinating mechanisms (similar to provisions contained in the joint regulations promulgated by the Commission and the Attorney General at part 42 of title 28 and part 1691 of title 29, Code of Federal Regulations, and the Memorandum of Understanding between the Commission and the Office of Federal Contract Compliance Programs dated January 16, 1981 (46 Fed. Reg. 7435, January 23, 1981) in regulations implementing this title and Rehabilitation Act of 1973 not later than 18 months after the date of enactment of this Act.

§ 12118. Effective date

[**Sec. 108**] This title shall become effective 24 months after the date of enactment.

TITLE III. Public Accommodations and Services Operated by Private Entities

Sec. 301. Definitions As used in this title:

(1) The term "commerce" means travel, trade, traffic, commerce, transportation, or communication—

(A) among the several States;

(B) between any foreign country or any territory or possession and any State; or

(C) between points in the same State but through another State or foreign country.

(2) The term "commercial facilities" means facilities—

(A) that are intended for nonresidential use; and

(B) whose operations will affect commerce.

Such term shall not include railroad locomotives, railroad freight cars, railroad cabooses, railroad cars described in section 242 or covered under this title, railroad rights-of-way, or facilities that are covered or expressly exempted from coverage under the Fair Housing Act of 1968 (42 U.S.C. 3601 *et seq.*).

(3) The term "demand responsive system" means any system of providing transportation of individuals by a vehicle, other than a system which is a fixed route system.

(4) The term "fixed route system" means a system of providing transportation of individuals (other than by aircraft) on which a vehicle is operated along a prescribed route according to a fixed schedule.

(5) The term "over-the-road bus" means a bus characterized by an elevated passenger deck located over a baggage compartment.

(6) The term "private entity" means any entity other than a public entity (as defined in section 201(1)).

(7) The following private entities are considered public accommodations for purposes of this title, if the operations of such entities affect commerce—

(A) an inn, hotel, motel, or other place of lodging, except for an establishment located within a building that contains not more than five rooms for rent or hire and that is actually occupied by the proprietor of such establishment as the residence of such proprietor;

(B) a restaurant, bar, or other establishment serving food or drink;

(C) a motion picture house, theater, concert hall, stadium, or other place of exhibition or entertainment;

(D) an auditorium, convention center, lecture hall, or other place of public gathering;

(E) a bakery, grocery store, clothing store, hardware store, shopping center, or other sales or rental establishment;

(F) a laundromat, dry-cleaner, bank, barber shop, beauty shop, travel service, shoe repair service, funeral parlor, gas station, office of an accountant or lawyer, pharmacy, insurance office, professional office of a health care provider, hospital, or other service establishment;

(G) a terminal, depot, or other station used for specified public transportation;

(H) a museum, library, gallery, or other place of public display or collection;

(I) a park, zoo, amusement park, or other place of recreation;

(J) a nursery, elementary, secondary, undergraduate, or postgraduate private school, or other place of education;

(K) a day care center, senior citizen center, homeless shelter, food bank, adoption agency, or other social service center establishment; and

(L) a gymnasium, health spa, bowling alley, golf course, or other place of exercise or recreation.

(8) The terms "rail" and "railroad" have the meaning given the term "railroad" in section 202(e) of the Federal Railroad Safety Act of 1970 (45 U.S.C. 431(e)).

(9) The term "readily achievable" means easily accomplishable and able to be carried out without much difficulty or expense. In determining whether an action is readily achievable, factors to be considered include—

(A) the nature and cost of the action needed under this Act;

(B) the overall financial resources of the facility or facilities involved in the action; the number of persons employed at such facility; the effect on expenses and resources, or the impact otherwise of such action upon the operation of the facility;

(C) the overall financial resources of the covered entity; the overall size of the business of a covered entity with respect to the number of its employees; the number, type, and location of its facilities; and

(D) the type of operation or operations of the covered entity, including the composition, structure, and functions of the workforce of such entity; the geographic separateness, administrative or fiscal relationship of the facility or facilities in question to the covered entity.

(10) The term "specified public transportation" means transporta-

tion by bus, rail, or any other conveyance (other than by aircraft) that provides the general public with general or special service (including charter service) on a regular and continuing basis.

(11) The term "vehicle" does not include a rail passenger car, railroad locomotive, railroad freight car, railroad caboose, or a railroad car described in section 242 or covered under this title.

Sec. 302. Prohibition of discrimination by public accommodation

(a) General Rule—No individual shall be discriminated against on the basis of disability in the full and equal enjoyment of the goods, services, facilities, privileges, advantages, or accommodations of any place of public accommodations by any person who owns, leases (or leases to), or operates a place of public accommodation.

(b) Construction—

(1) General prohibition—

(A) Activities—

(i) Denial of participation—It shall be discriminatory to subject an individual or class of individuals on the basis of a disability or disabilities of such individual or class, directly, or through contractual, licensing, or other arrangements, to a denial of the opportunity of the individual or class to participate in or benefit from the goods, services, facilities, privileges, advantages, or accommodations of an entity.

(ii) Participation in unequal benefit—It shall be discriminatory to afford an individual or class of individuals, on the basis of a disability or disabilities of such individual or class, directly, or through contractual, licensing, or other arrangements with the opportunity to participate in or benefit from a good, service, facility, privilege, advantage, or accommodation that is not equal to that afforded to other individuals.

(iii) Separate benefit—It shall be discriminatory to provide an individual or class of individuals, on the basis of a disability or disabilities of such individual or class, directly, or through contractual, licensing, or other arrangements with a good, service, facility, privilege, advantage, or accommodation that is different or separate from that provided to other individuals, unless such action is necessary to provide the individual or class of individuals with a good, service, facility, privilege, advantage, or accommodation, or other opportunity that is as effective as that provided to others.

(iv) Individual or class of individuals—For purposes of clauses (i) through (iii) of this subparagraph, the term "individual or class of individuals" refers to the clients or customers of the covered public accommodation that enters into the contractual, licensing or other arrangement.

(B) Integrated settings—Goods, services, facilities, privileges, advantages, and accommodations shall be afforded to an individual with a disability in the most integrated setting appropriate to the needs of the individual.

(C) Opportunity to participate—Notwithstanding the existence of separate or different programs or activities provided in accordance with this section, an individual with a disability shall not be denied the opportunity to participate in such programs or activities that are not separate or different.

(D) Administrative methods—An individual or entity shall not, directly or through contractual or other arrangements, utilize standards or criteria or methods of administration—

(i) that have the effect of discriminating on the basis of disability; or

(ii) that perpetuate the discrimination of others who are subject to common administrative control.

(E) Association—It shall be discriminatory to exclude or otherwise deny equal goods, services, facilities, privileges, advantages, accommodations, or other opportunities to an individual or entity because of the known disability of an individual with whom the individual or entity is known to have a relationship or association.
(2) Specific prohibitions—

(A) Discrimination—For purposes of subsection (a), discrimination includes—

(i) the imposition or application of eligibility criteria that screen out or tend to screen out an individual with a disability or any class of individuals with disabilities from fully and equally enjoying any goods, services, facilities, privileges, advantages, or accommodations, unless such criteria can be shown to be necessary for the provision of the goods, services, facilities, privileges, advantages, or accommodations being offered;

(ii) a failure to make reasonable modifications in policies, practices, or procedures, when such modifications are necessary to afford such goods, services, facilities, privileges, advantages, or accommodations to individuals with disabilities, unless the entity can demonstrate that making such modifications would fundamentally alter the nature of such goods, services, facilities, privileges, advantages, or accommodations;

(iii) a failure to take such steps as may be necessary to ensure that no individual with a disability is excluded, denied services, segregated or otherwise treated differently than other individuals because of the absence of auxiliary aids and services, unless the entity can demonstrate that taking such steps would fundamentally alter the nature of the good, service, facility, privilege, advantage, or accommodation being offered or would result in an undue burden;

(iv) a failure to remove architectural barriers, and communication barriers that are structural in nature, in existing facilities, and transportation barriers in existing vehicles and rail passenger cars used by an establishment for transporting individuals (not including barriers that can only be removed through the retrofitting of vehicles or rail passenger cars by the installation of a hydraulic or other lift), where such removal is readily achievable; and

(v) where an entity can demonstrate that the removal of a barrier under clause (iv) is not readily achievable, a failure to make such goods, services, facilities, privileges, advantages, or accommodations available through alternative methods if such methods are readily achievable.

(B) Fixed route system—

(i) Accessibility—It shall be considered discrimination for a private entity which operates a fixed route system and which is not subject to section 304 to purchase or lease a vehicle with a seating capacity in excess of 16 passengers (including the driver) for use on such system, for which a solicitation is made after the 30th day following the effective date of this subparagraph, that is not readily accessible to and usable by individuals with disabilities, including individuals who use wheelchairs.

(ii) Equivalent service—If a private entity which operates a fixed route system and which is not subject to section 304 purchases or leases a vehicle with a seating capacity of 16 passengers or less (including the driver) for use on such system after the effective date of this subparagraph that is not readily accessible to or usable by individuals with disabilities, it shall be considered discrimination for such entity to fail to operate such system so that, when viewed in its entirety, such system ensures a level of service to individuals with disabilities, including individuals who use wheelchairs, equivalent to the level of service provided to individuals without disabilities.

(C) Demand responsive system—For purposes of subsection (a), discrimination includes—

(i) a failure of a private entity which operates a demand responsive system and which is not subject to section 304 to operate such system so that, when viewed in its entirety, such system ensures a level of service to individuals with disabilities, including individuals who use wheelchairs, equivalent to the level of service provided to individuals without disabilities; and

(ii) the purchase or lease by such entity for use on such system of a vehicle with a seating capacity in excess of 16 passengers (including the driver), for which solicitations are made after the 30th day following the effective date of this subparagraph, that is not readily accessible to and usable by individuals with disabilities (including individuals who use wheelchairs) unless such entity can demonstrate that such system, when viewed in its entirety, provides a level of service to individuals with disabilities equivalent to that provided to individuals without disabilities.

(D) Over-the-road buses—

(i) Limitation on applicability—Subparagraphs (B) and (C) do not apply to over-the-road buses.

(ii) Accessibility requirements—For purposes of subsection (a), discrimination includes (I) the purchase or lease of an over-the-road bus which does not comply with the regulations issued under section 306 (a)(2) by a private entity which provides transportation of individuals and which is not primarily engaged in the business of transporting people, and (II) any other failure of such entity to comply with such regulations.

(3) Specific construction—Nothing in this title shall require an entity to permit an individual to participate in or benefit from the goods, services, facilities, privileges, advantages and accommodations of such entity where such individual poses a direct threat to the health or safety of others. The term "direct threat" means a significant risk to the health or safety of others that cannot be eliminated by a modification of policies, practices, or procedures or by the provision of auxiliary aids or services.

Sec. 303. New construction and alterations in public accommodations and commercial facilities

(a) Application of term—Except as provided in subsection (b), as applied to public accommodations and commercial facilities, discrimination for purposes of section 302(a) includes—

(1) a failure to design and construct facilities for first occupancy later than 30 months after the date of enactment of this Act that are readily accessible to and usable by individuals with disabilities, except where an entity can demonstrate that it is structurally impracticable to meet the requirements of such subsection in accordance with standards set forth or incorporated by reference in regulations issued under this title; and

(2) with respect to a facility or part thereof that is altered by, on behalf of, or for the use of an establishment in a manner that affects or could affect the usability of the facility or part thereof, a failure to make alterations in such a manner that, to the maximum extent feasible, the altered portions of the facility are readily accessible to and usable by individuals with disabilities, including individuals who use wheelchairs. Where the entity is undertaking an alteration that affects or could affect usability of or access to an area of the facility containing a primary function, the entity shall also make the alterations in such a manner that, to the maximum extent feasible, the path of travel to the altered area and the bathrooms, telephones, and drinking fountains serving the altered area, are readily accessible to and usable by individuals with disabilities where such alterations to the path of travel or the bathrooms, telephones, and drinking fountains serving the altered area are not disproportionate to the overall alterations in terms of cost and scope (as determined under criteria established by the Attorney General).

(b) Elevator—Subsection (a) shall not be construed to require the installation of an elevator for facilities that are less than three stories or have less than 3,000 square feet per story unless the building is a shopping center, a shopping mall, or the professional office of a health care provider or unless the Attorney General determines that a particular category of such facilities requires the installation of elevators based on the usage of such facilities.

Sec. 304. Prohibition of discrimination in specified public transportation services provided by private entities

(a) General Rule—No individual shall be discriminated against on the basis of disability in the full and equal enjoyment of specified public transportation services provided by a private entity that is primarily engaged in the business of transporting people and whose operations affect commerce.

(b) Construction—For purposes of subsection (a), discrimination includes—

(1) the imposition or application by a entity described in subsection (a) of eligibility criteria that screen out or tend to screen out an individ-

ual with a disability or any class of individuals with disabilities from fully enjoying the specified public transportation services provided by the entity, unless such criteria can be shown to be necessary for the provision of the services being offered;

(2) the failure of such entity to—

(A) make reasonable modifications consistent with those required under section 302(b)(2)(A)(ii);

(B) provide auxiliary aids and services consistent with the requirements of section 302(b)(2)(A)(iii); and

(C) remove barriers consistent with the requirements of section 302(b)(2)(A) and with the requirements of section 303(a)(2);

(3) the purchase or lease by such entity of a new vehicle (other than an automobile, a van with a seating capacity of less than 8 passengers, including the driver, or an over-the-road bus) which is to be used to provide specified public transportation and for which a solicitation is made after the 30th day following the effective date of this section, that is not readily accessible to and usable by individuals with disabilities, including individuals who use wheelchairs; except that the new vehicle need not be readily accessible to and usable by such individuals if the new vehicle is to be used solely in a demand responsive system and if the entity can demonstrate that such system, when viewed in its entirety, provides a level of service to such individuals equivalent to the level of service provided to the general public;

(4)(A) the purchase or lease by such entity of an over-the-road bus which does not comply with the regulations issued under section 306(a)(2); and

(B) any other failure of such entity to comply with such regulations; and

(5) the purchase or lease by such entity of a new van with a seating capacity of less than 8 passengers, including the driver, which is to be used to provide specified public transportation and for which a solicitation is made after the 30th day following the effective date of this section that is not readily accessible to or usable by individuals with disabilities, including individuals who use wheelchairs; except that the new van need not be readily accessible to and usable by such individuals if the entity can demonstrate that the system for which the van is being purchased or leased, when viewed in its entirety, provides a level of service to such individuals equivalent to the level of service provided to the general public;

(6) the purchase or lease by such entity of a new rail passenger car that is to be used to provide specified public transportation, and for

which a solicitation is made later than 30 days after the effective date of this paragraph, that is not readily accessible to and usable by individuals with disabilities, including individuals who use wheelchairs; and

(7) the remanufacture by such entity of a rail passenger car that is to be used to provide specified public transportation so as to extend its usable life for 10 years or more, or the purchase or lease by such entity of such a rail car, unless the rail car, to the maximum extent feasible, is made readily accessible to and usable by individuals with disabilities, including individuals who use wheelchairs.

(c) Historical or antiquated cars—

(1) Exception—To the extent that compliance with subsection (b)(2)(C) or (b)(7) would significantly alter the historic or antiquated character of a historical or antiquated rail passenger car, or a rail station served exclusively by such cars, or would result in violation of any rule, regulation, standard, or order issued by the Secretary of Transportation under the Federal Railroad Safety Act of 1970, such compliance shall not be required.

(2) Definition—As used in this subsection, the term "historical or antiquated rail passenger car" means a rail passenger car—

(A) which is not less than 30 years old at the time of its use for transporting individuals;

(B) the manufacturer of which is no longer in the business of manufacturing rail passenger cars; and

(C) which—

(i) has a consequential association with events or persons significant to the past; or

(ii) embodies, or is being restored to embody, the distinctive characteristics of a type of rail passenger car used in the past, or to represent a time period which has passed.

Sec. 305. Study

(a) Purposes—The Office of Technology Assessment shall undertake a study to determine—

(1) the access needs of individuals with disabilities to over-the-road buses and over-the-road bus service; and

(2) the most cost-effective methods for providing access to over-the-road buses and over-the-road bus service to individuals with disabilities, particularly individuals who use wheelchairs, through all forms of boarding options.

(b) Contents—The study shall include, at a minimum, an analysis of the following:

(1) The anticipated demand by individuals with disabilities for accessible over-the-road buses and over-the-road bus service.

(2) The degree to which such buses and service, including any service required under sections 304(b)(4) and 306(a)(2), are readily accessible to and usable by individuals with disabilities.

(3) The effectiveness of various methods of providing accessibility to such buses and service to individuals with disabilities.

(4) The cost of providing accessible over-the-road buses and bus service to individuals with disabilities, including consideration of recent technological and cost saving developments in equipment and devices.

(5) Possible design changes in over-the-road buses that could enhance accessibility, including the installation of accessible restrooms which do not result in a loss of seating capacity.

(6) The impact of accessibility requirements on the continuation of over-the-road bus service, with particular consideration of the impact of such requirements on such service to rural communities.

(c) Advisory committee—In conducting the study required by subsection (a), the Office of Technology Assessment shall establish an advisory committee, which shall consist of—

(1) members selected from among private operators and manufacturers of over-the-road buses;

(2) members selected from among individuals with disabilities, particularly individuals who use wheelchairs, who are potential riders of such buses; and

(3) members selected for their technical expertise on issues included in the study, including manufacturers of boarding assistance equipment and devices.

The number of members selected under each of paragraphs (1) and (2) shall be equal, and the total number of members selected under paragraphs (1) and (2) shall exceed the number of members selected under paragraph (3).

(d) Deadline—The study required by subsection (a), along with recommendations by the Office of Technology Assessment, including any policy options for legislative action, shall be submitted to the President and Congress within 36 months after the date of the enactment of this Act. If the President determines that compliance with the regulations issued pursuant to section 306(a)(2)(B) on or before the applicable deadlines specified in section 306(a)(2)(B) will result in a significant reduction in intercity over-the-road bus service, the President shall extend each such deadline by 1 year.

(e) Review—In developing the study required by subsection (a), the Office of Technology Assessment shall provide a preliminary draft of such study to the Architectural and Transportation Barriers Compliance Board established under section 502 of the Rehabilitation Act of 1973 (29 U.S.C. 792). The Board shall have an opportunity to comment on such draft study, and any such comments by the Board made in writing within 120 days after the Board's receipt of the draft study shall be incorporated as part of the final study required to be submitted under subsection (d).

Sec. 306. Regulations

(a) Transportation Provisions—

(1) General rule—Not later than 1 year after the date of the enactment of this Act, the Secretary of Transportation shall issue regulations in an accessible format to carry out sections 302(b)(2)(B) and (C) and to carry out section 304 (other than subsection (b)(4)).

(2) Special rules for providing access to over-the-road buses—

(A) Interim requirements—

(i) Issuance—Not later than 1 year after the date of the enactment of this Act, the Secretary of Transportation shall issue regulations in an accessible format to carry out sections 304(b)(4) and 302(b)(2)(D)(ii) that require each private entity which uses an over-the-road bus to provide transportation of individuals to provide accessibility to such bus; except that such regulations shall not require any structural changes in over-the-road buses in order to provide access to individuals who use wheelchairs during the effective period of such regulations and shall not require the purchase of boarding assistance devices to provide access to such individuals.

(ii) Effective period—The regulations issued pursuant to this subparagraph shall be effective until the effective date of the regulations issued under subparagraph (B).

(B) Final requirement—

(i) Review of study and interim requirements—The Secretary shall review the study submitted under section 305 and the regulations issued pursuant to subparagraph (A).

(ii) Issuance—Not later than 1 year after the date of the submission of the study under section 305, the Secretary shall issue in an accessible format new regulations to carry out sections 304(b)(4) and 302(b)(2)(D)(ii) that require, taking into account the purposes of the study under section 305 and any recommendations resulting from such study, each private entity which uses an over-the-road bus to provide transportation to individuals to provide accessibility to such bus to individuals with disabilities, including individuals who use wheelchairs.

(iii) Effective period—Subject to section 305 (d), the regulations issued pursuant to this subparagraph shall take effect—

(I) with respect to small providers of transportation (as defined by the Secretary), 7 years after the date of the enactment of this Act; and

(II) with respect to other providers of transportation, 6 years after such date of enactment.

(C) Limitation on requiring installation of accessible restrooms—The regulations issued pursuant to this paragraph shall not require the installation of accessible restrooms in over-the-road buses if such installation would result in a loss of seating capacity.

(3) Standards—The regulations issued pursuant to this subsection shall include standards applicable to facilities and vehicles covered by sections 302(b)(2) and 304.

(b) Other provisions—Not later than 1 year after the date of the enactment of this Act, the Attorney General shall issue regulations in an accessible format to carry out the provisions of this title not referred to in subsection (a) that include standards applicable to facilities and vehicles covered under section 302.

(c) Consistency With ATBCB Guidelines—Standards included in regulations issued under subsections (a) and (b) shall be consistent with the minimum guidelines and requirements issued by the Architectural and Transportation Barriers Compliance Board in accordance with section 504 of this Act.

(d) Interim Accessibility Standards—

(1) Facilities—If final regulations have not been issued pursuant to this section, for new construction or alterations for which a valid and appropriate State or local building permit is obtained prior to the issuance of final regulations under this section, and for which the construction or alteration authorized by such permit begins within one year of the receipt of such permit and is completed under the terms of such permit, compliance with the Uniform Federal Accessibility Standards in effect at the time the building permit is issued shall suffice to satisfy the requirement that facilities be readily accessible to and usable by persons with disabilities as required under section 303, except that, if such final regulations have not been issued one year after the Architectural and Transportation Barriers Compliance Board has issued the supplemental minimum guidelines required under section 504(a) of this Act, compli-

ance with such supplemental minimum guidelines shall be necessary to satisfy the requirement that facilities be readily accessible to and usable by persons with disabilities prior to issuance of the final regulations.

(2) Vehicles and rail passenger cars—If final regulations have not been issued pursuant to this section, a private entity shall be considered to have complied with the requirements of this title, if any, that a vehicle or rail passenger car be readily accessible to and usable by individuals with disabilities, if the design for such vehicle or car complies with the laws and regulations (including the Minimum Guidelines and Requirements for Accessible Design and such supplemental minimum guidelines as are issued under section 504(a) of this Act) governing accessibility of such vehicles or cars, to the extent that such laws and regulations are not inconsistent with this title and are in effect at the time such design is substantially completed.

Sec. 307. Exemptions for private clubs and religious organizations

The provisions of this title shall not apply to private clubs or establishments exempted from coverage under title II of the Civil Rights Act of 1964 (42 U.S.C. 2000-a(e)) or to religious organizations or entities controlled by religious organizations, including places of worship.

Sec. 308. Enforcement

(a) In general.

(1) Availability of remedies and procedures.—The remedies and procedures set forth in section 204(a) of the Civil Rights Act of 1964 (42 U.S.C. 2000a-3(a)) are the remedies and procedures this title provides to any person who is being subjected to discrimination on the basis of disability in violation of this title or who has reasonable grounds for believing that such person is about to be subjected to discrimination in violation of section 303. Nothing in this section shall require a person with a disability to engage in a futile gesture if such person has actual notice that a person or organization covered by this title does not intend to comply with its provisions.

(2) Injunctive relief—In the case of violations of section 302(b)(2)(A)(iv) and section 303(a), injunctive relief shall include an order to alter facilities to make such facilities readily accessible to and usable by individuals with disabilities to the extent required by this title. Where appropriate, injunctive relief shall also include requiring the provision of an auxiliary aid or service, modification of a policy, or provision of alternative methods, to the extent required by this title.

(b) Enforcement by the attorney general—

(1) Denial of rights—

(A) Duty to investigate—

(i) In general—The Attorney General shall investigate alleged violations of this title, and shall undertake periodic reviews of compliance of covered entities under this title.

(ii) Attorney general certification—On the application of a State or local government, the Attorney General may, in consultation with the Architectural and Transportation Barriers Compliance Board, and after prior notice and a public hearing at which persons, including individuals with disabilities, are provided an opportunity to testify against such certification, certify that a State law or local building code or similar ordinance that establishes accessibility requirements meets or exceeds the minimum requirements of this Act for the accessibility and usability of covered facilities under this title. At any enforcement proceeding under this section, such certification by the Attorney General shall be rebuttable evidence that such State law or local ordinance does meet or exceed the minimum requirements of this Act.

(B) Potential violation—If the Attorney General has reasonable cause to believe that—

(i) any person or group of persons is engaged in a pattern or practice of discrimination under this title; or

(ii) any person or group of persons has been discriminated against under this title and such discrimination raises an issue of general public importance, the Attorney General may commence a civil action in any appropriate United States district court.

(2) Authority of court—In a civil action under paragraph (1)(B), the court—

(A) may grant any equitable relief that such court considers to be appropriate, including, to the extent required by this title—

(i) granting temporary, preliminary, or permanent relief;

(ii) providing an auxiliary aid or service, modification of policy, practice, or procedure, or alternative method; and

(iii) making facilities readily accessible to and usable by individuals with disabilities;

(B) may award such other relief as the court considers to be appropriate, including monetary damages to persons aggrieved when requested by the Attorney General; and

(C) may, to vindicate the public interest, assess a civil penalty against the entity in an amount—

(i) not exceeding $50,000 for a first violation; and

(ii) not exceeding $100,000 for any subsequent violation.

(3) Single violation—For purposes of paragraph (2)(C), in determining whether a first or subsequent violation has occurred, a determination in a single action, by judgment or settlement, that the covered entity has engaged in more than one discriminatory act shall be counted as a single violation.

(4) Punitive damages—For purposes of subsection (b)(2)(B), the term "monetary damages" and "such other relief" does not include punitive damages.

(5) Judicial consideration—In a civil action under paragraph (1)(B), the court, when considering what amount of civil penalty, if any, is appropriate, shall give consideration to any good faith effort or attempt to comply with this Act by the entity. In evaluating good faith, the court shall consider, among other factors it deems relevant, whether the entity could have reasonably anticipated the need for an appropriate type of auxiliary aid needed to accommodate the unique needs of a particular individual with a disability.

Sec. 309. Examinations and courses

Any person that offers examinations or courses related to applications, licensing, certification, or credentialing for secondary or post-secondary education, professional, or trade purposes shall offer such examinations or courses in a place and manner accessible to persons with disabilities or offer alternative accessible arrangements for such individuals.

Sec. 310. Effective date

(a) General Rule—Except as provided in subsections (b) and (c), this title shall become effective 18 months after the date of the enactment of this Act.

(b) Civil Actions—Except for any civil action brought for a violation of section 303, no civil action shall be brought for any act or omission described in section 302 which occurs—

(1) during the first 6 months after the effective date, against businesses that employ 25 or fewer employees and have gross receipts of $1,000,000 or less; and

(2) during the first year after the effective date, against businesses that employ 10 or fewer employees and have gross receipts of $500,000 or less.

(c) Exception—Sections 302(a) for purposes of section 302(b)(2)(B) and (C) only, 304(a) for purposes of section 304(b)(3) only, 304(b)(3), 305, and 306 shall take effect on the date of the enactment of this Act.

Index